SIMPLE
HONEST
FOOD

SIMPLE
HONEST
FOOD

The Best of Bill Granger

LYONS PRESS
Guilford, Connecticut
An imprint of Globe Pequot Press

contents

introduction

I come from a family of butchers and bakers so it's fair to say that food, in some shape or form, was always going to be my destiny. Food is what gives my life rhythm. From healthy family breakfasts, to special Saturday night dinners for friends, or seeing my daughters' faces light up when I take a tray of cookies out of the oven, my week revolves around the endless pleasures of good food.

Some days I cook for pleasure and some days for fuel. In today's world we are bombarded with so much of everything when what we really need is very simple — our health and time to enjoy our friends, loved ones and ourselves. Food anchors all the parts of my life. What I cook each day is dependent on many different factors: time, energy levels, what's in the shops.

On holiday in Paris, I had the luxury of shopping daily at local markets, buying some of the most beautiful produce I've ever seen — blueberries with flavour, pink and white radishes the size of my little finger, just-picked herbs and salad greens, amazing cheeses that just oozed — really extraordinary. While I'd love to be able to shop and cook like this every day, it's not realistic given my increasingly busy life. Sometimes there's barely enough time for a quick trip to the supermarket, but I never let this become a barrier to cooking, or let the job of preparing dinner every day become tedious.

The meal I prepare on a Monday night is different to the celebration lunch I make for friends, but all my food is similarly pared back. The greatest sophistication is in simplicity, and the ability to create good food is one of life's most reassuring skills and is immensely satisfying. I hope these recipes inspire you.

breakfast

Early morning is my favorite time of day, always has been. I love waking up early and pottering in the kitchen while it's still dark outside ... there's something very comforting and nurturing about it.

I'm always amazed at people who don't eat breakfast. I love breakfasts — maybe that's why my restaurants have become well known for them. As far as I can see, if you eat a good breakfast you've done a third of your day's work for eating well. It's pretty simple logic.

I make an effort to have breakfast with my family. We usually all decide on our breakfast, whether it be buckwheat pancakes or soft-boiled eggs or whatever, and we all share in its preparation while getting ready for the day. I can't wait until my girls are old enough to bring me breakfast in bed, but until that time comes we usually have a gang of friends over on a Sunday morning.

As long as it's fresh, it doesn't matter what you serve. Relax, just pop the food and a big jug of juice in the middle of the table and let people help themselves. Remember, you are not a restaurant — and it's about the company after all!

buttermilk pancakes

2 cups all-purpose flour
1 tablespoon baking powder
a pinch of salt
2½ tablespoons sugar
2 eggs, lightly beaten
3 cups buttermilk
2½ oz unsalted butter, melted
unsalted butter, extra, for greasing the pan

to serve
caramelized plums (see below)
maple syrup
yogurt

Stir the flour, baking powder, salt and sugar together in a bowl. Add the egg, buttermilk and melted butter and whisk to combine.

Heat a large non-stick frying pan over a medium heat and brush a small portion of butter over the base. For each pancake, ladle ⅓ cup of batter into the pan and cook for about 2 minutes, until bubbles appear on the surface. Turn the pancakes over and cook for another minute. Transfer to a plate and keep warm while cooking the rest of the pancakes.

Serve the pancakes in stacks with the plums, a jug of maple syrup and some yogurt.

To caramelize plums, heat a frying pan over a high heat, cut the plums in half and remove the pits, sprinkle the cut sides with sugar and put the plums in the hot frying pan with the cut side down. Sear the plums until the sugar melts and caramelizes. This should take about a minute.

mushrooms on toast

SERVES 4

1½ oz unsalted butter, chilled and cubed

4 teaspoons olive oil, plus extra, for brushing

2 garlic cloves, finely chopped

1 lb 2 oz mixed small mushrooms, such as button and Swiss brown, halved

sea salt

freshly ground black pepper

1 teaspoon balsamic vinegar

2½ tablespoons chopped fresh Italian parsley

1 teaspoon chopped fresh tarragon

1 teaspoon grated lemon zest

4 slices sourdough bread

1 garlic clove, extra, for rubbing on bread

1 cup ricotta cheese

Put half the butter with the oil and chopped garlic in a saucepan over a medium to high heat. Add the mushrooms, ¼ cup water and salt and pepper, to taste. Cover and cook, stirring occasionally, for about 15 minutes, or until the mushrooms are cooked and the liquid is syrupy. Stir in the balsamic vinegar, parsley, tarragon and lemon zest. Taste for seasoning and adjust if necessary. Whisk the remaining cold butter through to thicken the mushroom sauce.

Brush the bread on both sides with the extra olive oil. Broil until golden on both sides, cut the extra garlic clove, then rub both sides of the bread with the garlic and place on serving plates. Top with ricotta cheese and then mushrooms and serve immediately.

Mushrooms keep best if you store them in a brown paper bag to allow them to breathe. Keeping them in plastic causes them to sweat.

17

french toast with fresh berry sauce

3 eggs
¾ cup milk
8 thick slices brioche or panettone
I oz unsalted butter

to serve
fresh berry sauce (see below)
confectioners' sugar, for sprinkling

Whisk the eggs and milk together in a bowl to combine. Place the brioche or panettone in a shallow dish and pour the milk mixture over the top. Allow the milk to soak in thoroughly, then turn the bread over and soak the other side — if you are using panettone it will need to be soaked for a little longer because it is drier.

Heat a large non-stick frying pan over a medium to high heat and melt half of the butter. Add four slices of bread to the pan and fry for about 1 minute, until golden. Turn over and cook until the other side is golden. Repeat with the remaining butter and bread.

Serve immediately with the berry sauce, remaining berries and a sprinkling of icing sugar.

FRESH BERRY SAUCE

2 cups raspberries or mixed berries
¼ cup superfine sugar
4 teaspoons lemon juice

Put half the berries in a blender with the sugar and lemon juice. Purée until smooth, then pour into a bowl.

18

bircher muesli with pear and blueberries

SERVES 4

2 cups mixed old-fashioned oats,
barley and rye
1½ cups pear juice
2 pears, skin left on and grated
½ cup plain yogurt
⅓ cup toasted chopped almonds
½ cup blueberries

Put the old-fashioned oats, barley and rye in a bowl with the pear juice and leave to soak for 1 hour, or overnight, in the refrigerator. Add the grated pear and yogurt and mix well. Spoon the muesli into serving bowls and top each with the toasted almonds and blueberries.

The quickest and easiest way to toast nuts is to dry-fry them in a frying pan over a medium heat. However, don't walk away from them because they burn very quickly.

bill's eggs

FRIED

2 teaspoons olive oil
2 eggs, at room temperature
sea salt
freshly ground black pepper

Place a large non-stick frying pan over a medium to high heat for 1 minute. Add the olive oil and swirl until the base of the pan is evenly coated. Carefully crack the eggs into the pan and sprinkle with salt and pepper. Cook for 1 minute. If you like the yolks of your eggs harder, cover the pan with a lid and cook for another minute. Serve with sourdough or whole wheat toast and spicy tomato relish (see page 47).

SCRAMBLED

2 eggs, at room temperature
1/3 cup cream
a pinch of salt
1/4 oz butter

Place the eggs, cream and salt in a bowl and whisk together. Put the butter in a non-stick frying pan over a high heat. Once the butter is melted, pour in the egg mixture and cook for 20 seconds, or until it begins to set around the edge. Using a wooden spoon, stir and bring the egg mixture on the edge of the pan into the center. It is important to fold the eggs, not scramble them. Leave for 20 seconds, then repeat the folding process. When the eggs are just set, turn out onto a plate and serve with sourdough or wholemeal toast.

BOILED

Place a saucepan of water over a high heat and bring to a boil. Gently place your eggs, which should be at room temperature, into the water then adjust the heat until the water is simmering. For a soft-boiled egg, cook for 4 minutes, medium-boiled 5–6 minutes and hard-boiled 10 minutes.

POACHED

Fill a shallow frying pan with water until it is 2 inches deep and place over a high heat. Once the water boils, turn off the heat and break the eggs directly into the water. Crack the shells open at the water surface so the eggs simply slide into the water. Cover with a tight-fitting lid and leave to cook for 3 minutes, or until the egg whites are opaque. Remove from the pan with a slotted spoon and drain on a clean dish towel.

23

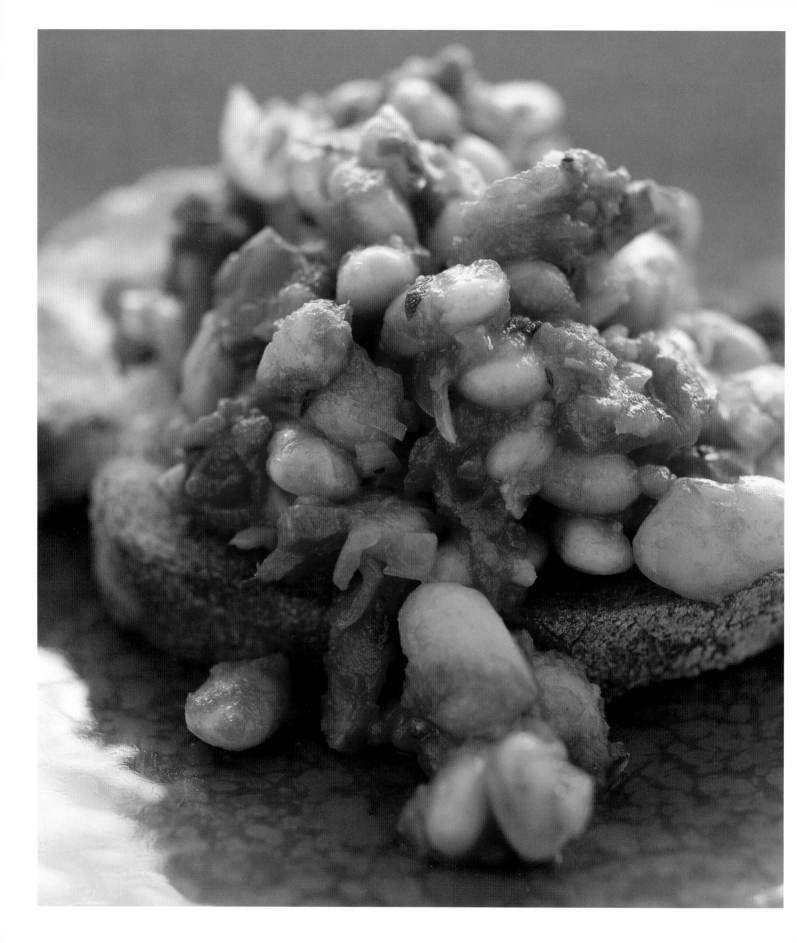

fresh
baked beans

4 teaspoons olive oil
1 onion, finely chopped
3½ oz pancetta, chopped
1 garlic clove, crushed
2 anchovies, chopped
1 teaspoon fresh thyme leaves, finely chopped
½ teaspoon dried oregano
14 oz can chopped tomaotes
2 x 14 oz cans cannellini beans, rinsed
sea salt
freshly ground black pepper

Preheat the oven to 315°F. Heat the olive oil in a large flameproof casserole dish over a medium heat. Add the onion and cook, stirring for 5–6 minutes until the onion is soft. Add the pancetta and cook, stirring occasionally, for 5 minutes, or until slightly crisp. Add the garlic, anchovies, thyme and oregano and cook, stirring, for another minute.

Add the tomatoes and ½ cup of water, bring to a boil and then reduce the heat to simmer for 10 minutes. Stir in the beans, put a lid on the casserole dish and bake in the oven for 30 minutes. Season with salt and pepper.

baked eggs with spinach and parmesan

SERVES 4

4 teaspoons olive oil
7 oz baby spinach leaves
sea salt
freshly ground black pepper
8 eggs
$\frac{1}{3}$ cup cream
$\frac{1}{3}$ cup coarsley grated parmesan cheese

to serve
toast

Preheat the oven to 400°F. Lightly grease four 3½ inch ramekins and place on a baking tray.

Heat a saucepan or frying pan over a medium heat. Add the oil to the pan, then add the spinach and season with salt and pepper. Cook until the leaves are just softened. Drain the spinach in a colander and, as soon as it's cool enough to handle, squeeze out the excess liquid.

Spoon the spinach into the ramekins and break 2 eggs into each ramekin on top of the spinach.

Pour ¼ of the cream over each serving of the eggs and sprinkle with ¼ of the parmesan. Bake for 15 minutes, or until the eggs are set and puffed up. Season and serve immediately with toast.

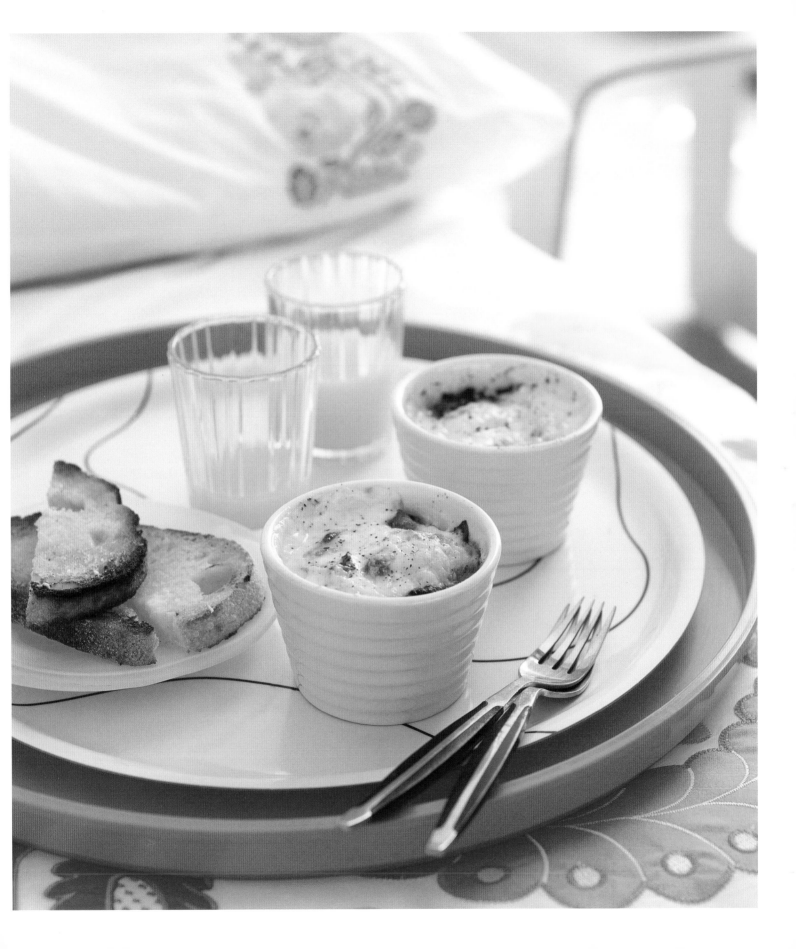

blueberry and almond toasted muesli

3 cups old-fashioned oats
½ cup apple juice
2½ tablespoons vegetable oil
½ cup raw almonds
1 cup sunflower seeds
¼ cup pumpkin seeds
¼ cup sesame seeds
½ cup flaked coconut
1 cup dried blueberries
(if you can't get these, use currants
or raisins or a mixture of both)

to serve
raspberry swirl yogurt (see below)
nectarines, pitted and cut into wedges
milk

Preheat the oven to 315°F. Place all the ingredients, except for the dried blueberries, in a large bowl and stir well to combine. Spread the mixture evenly over a large baking tray and place in the oven for 30 minutes, stirring occasionally until lightly browned.

Remove from the oven, allow to cool then add the blueberries. This muesli can be stored in an airtight container for up to 1 month. Serve with the raspberry swirl yogurt, nectarines and milk.

To make raspberry swirl yogurt, just mash ½ cup of raspberries with a fork and lightly ripple through a cup of plain yogurt.

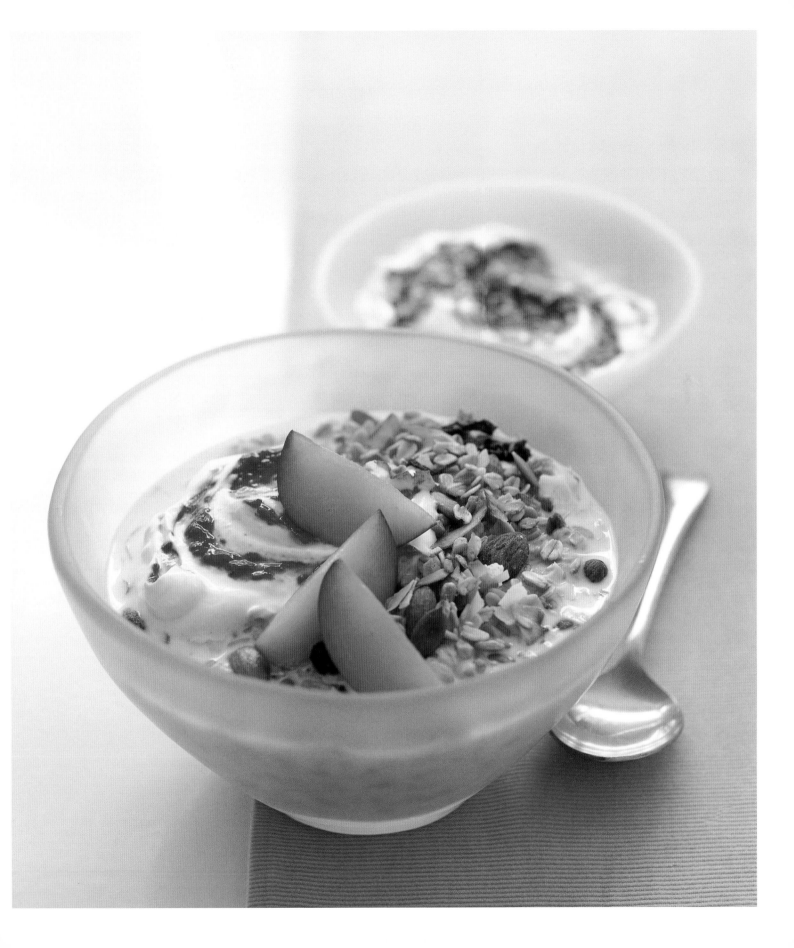

five-grain oatmeal with brown sugar peaches

SERVES 4

2½ cups of mixed grains such as old-
fashioned oats, rice,
barley, triticale or kibbled rye
(some health food shops sell a
five-grain mix which I think is ideal)
2½ cups boiling water
2½ cups milk
3 peaches, quartered
⅓ cup soft brown sugar

to serve
brown sugar, extra
warmed milk

Preheat the oven to 400°F. Place the grains and boiling water in a saucepan and stir to combine. Leave for 10 minutes. Add the milk and stir again. Place over a medium heat and slowly bring to a boil. Reduce the heat and simmer for 10 minutes, stirring often.

Meanwhile, place the peaches on a baking tray and sprinkle with the brown sugar. Bake in the oven for about 15 minutes, or until the fruit has softened and slightly caramelized.

Spoon the porridge into serving bowls and top with the peaches. Serve with brown sugar and a jug of warmed milk.

When fresh peaches are out of season you can use dried peaches or other dried fruit by soaking them in boiling water for 5 minutes. Make up more than you need of the grain mix and store in an airtight container for up to 2 months.

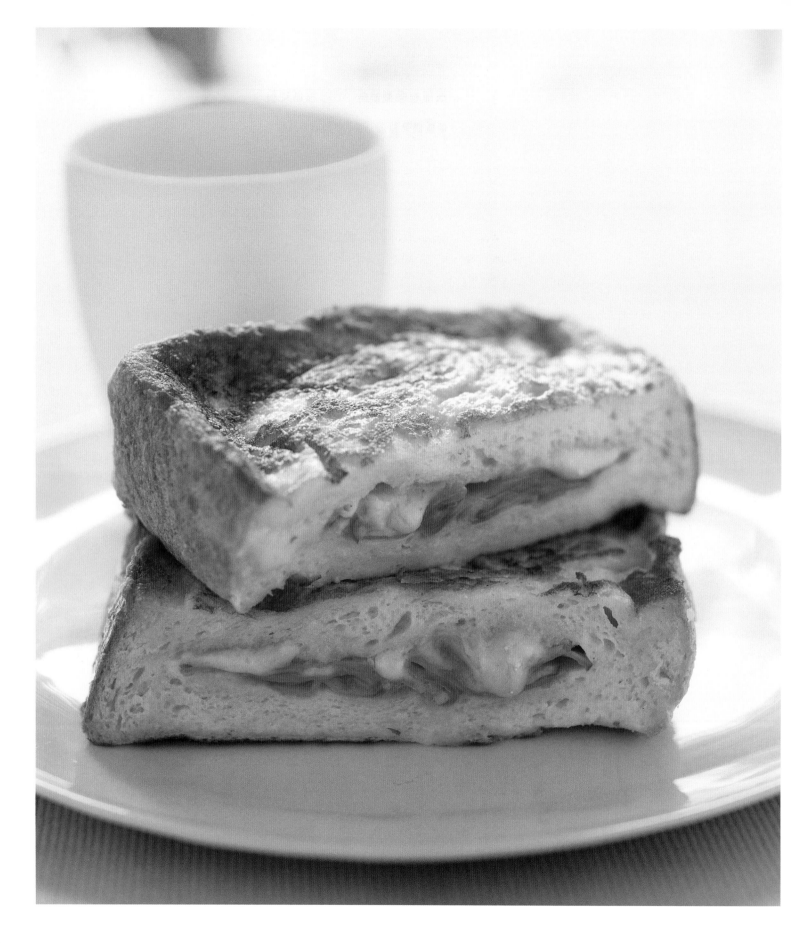

ham and gruyère french toast

4 eggs
¾ cup milk
sea salt
freshly ground black pepper
4 slices white bread, 1¼ inch thick
2 teaspoons dijon mustard
4 slices leg ham, trimmed to fit bread
4 slices gruyère cheese, trimmed
to fit bread
4 teaspoons olive oil

Preheat the oven to 350°F. Place the eggs, milk, salt and pepper into a large bowl. Whisk to combine.

With a sharp, thin-bladed knife, carefully slit open one side of each slice of bread to form a pocket, leaving ½ inch around the edges. Spread the mustard on one side of the pocket and place a slice of ham and cheese inside. Put the pockets into a shallow dish. Pour over the egg mixture and leave for 5 minutes, turning once.

Heat a non-stick frying pan over a medium to high heat, add half of the olive oil and swirl to coat the base of the pan. Add two bread pockets, cook on one side for about 2 minutes until golden brown, turn and cook for another minute. Remove from the pan and place on a baking tray. Repeat with the remaining oil and bread pockets. Place the baking tray in the oven and cook for 10 minutes, or until hot and the cheese has melted.

oat, pear and raspberry loaf

MAKES 8 TO 10 SLICES

topping

¼ cup old-fashioned oats

¼ cup soft brown sugar

2½ tablespoons all-purpose flour

1 oz chilled butter, cut into small pieces

cake

1 cup old-fashioned oats

1½ cups boiling water

5½ oz unsalted butter, diced

½ cup soft brown sugar

¼ cup superfine sugar

2 eggs

1 teaspoon natural vanilla extract

1½ cups all-purpose flour

a pinch of sea salt

1 teaspoon baking powder

2 ripe pears, peeled, cored and diced

½ cup raspberries, fresh or frozen

to serve

butter

Preheat the oven to 350°F. To make the topping, place all the ingredients into a bowl and rub the butter into the mixture with your fingertips until well incorporated and small clumps form.

To make the cake, place the oats into a bowl and pour over the boiling water. Stir and leave to cool until lukewarm. Cream the butter and sugars in a bowl until pale and creamy. Add the eggs, one at a time, beating well after each addition. Mix in the vanilla. Sift the flour, sea salt and baking powder into the bowl. Drain any excess water off the oats. Add the oats to the mixture and fold to combine. Spread two-thirds of the mixture into a greased or non-stick 7½ x 4¼ inch loaf pan. Sprinkle with the pears and raspberries, top with the remaining cake batter then sprinkle the topping over evenly.

Bake for 1 hour 10 minutes, or until a skewer inserted into the center of the cake comes out clean. Turn out onto a plate before quickly transferring to a wire rack with the topping facing upwards. Leave to cool slightly before cutting. Serve in slices with butter.

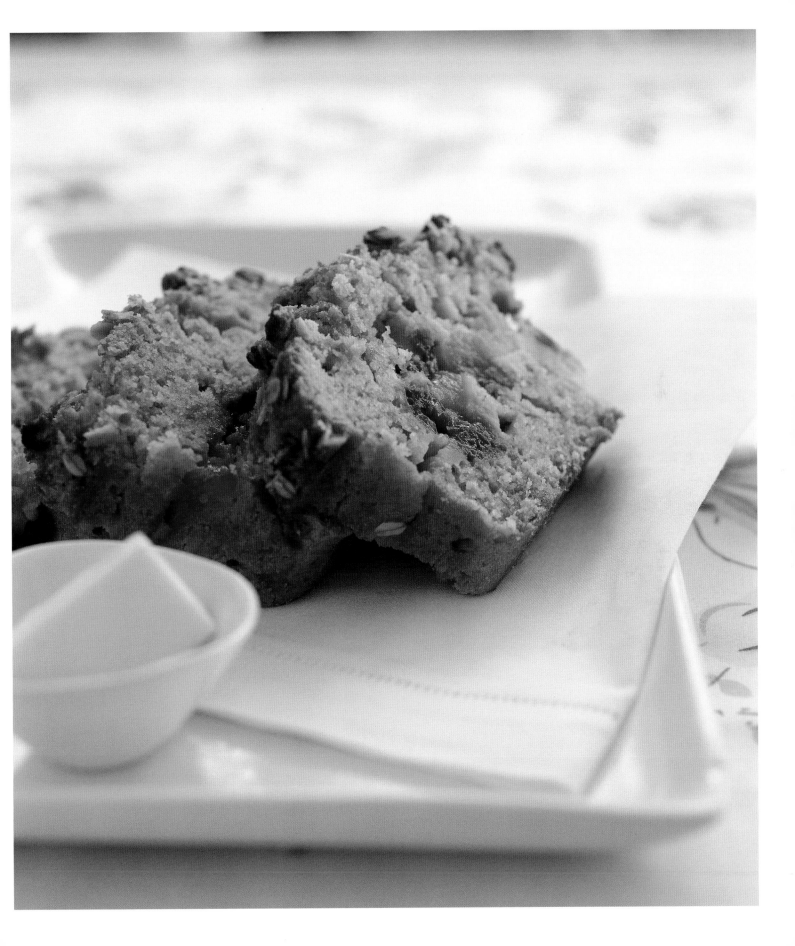

mango lassi

½ cup plain yogurt
½ cup orange juice
1 mango, peeled and cubed
3 large ice cubes

Place all the ingredients in a blender and blend until the mango is well combined. Pour into a tall glass and serve.

raspberry and strawberry smoothie

MAKES 1

4 strawberries, hulled
¼ cup raspberries
½ oz plain yogurt
½ cup milk
3–4 large ice cubes

Place all the ingredients in a blender and blend until smooth. Pour into a tall glass and serve.

real muesli bars

3½ cups old-fashioned oats
½ cup shredded coconut
½ cup flaked almonds
½ cup wheatgerm
¼ cup sesame seeds
¼ cup sunflower seeds
⅓ cup chopped dried apricots
¾ cup honey
¼ cup soft brown sugar
½ cup vegetable oil

Preheat the oven to 250°F. Lightly grease and line a 14 x 10 inch baking pan with parchment paper. Put the oats, coconut, almonds, wheatgerm, sesame seeds, sunflower seeds and apricots in a bowl.

Put the honey, sugar and oil in a small saucepan and stir over medium heat until the sugar has dissolved. Pour this over the dry ingredients in the bowl and stir until everything is well combined, mixing with your hands if necessary.

Press the mixture into the pan and bake for 50 minutes, or until golden brown. Cut into bars while still warm.

berry yogurt muffins

MAKES 12

1½ cups self-rising flour
1 cup whole-wheat self-rising flour
1 teaspoon ground cinnamon
¾ cup soft brown sugar
1 cup buttermilk
½ cup low-fat plain yogurt
2 eggs, lightly beaten
2½ tablespoons vegetable oil
2 cups chopped mixed berries (I like strawberries and raspberries)

Preheat the oven to 350°F. Line a 12-hole ½ cup capacity muffin pan with paper cups.

Sift the two flours and cinnamon together into a large bowl. Stir in the sugar and then make a well in the center. Place the buttermilk, yogurt, eggs and oil into a large bowl and whisk with a fork until just combined. Pour into the well in the dry ingredients and stir with a wooden spoon.

Fold the berries through the mixture (do not overmix or your muffins will be tough). Spoon into the muffin pan and bake for 20 minutes, or until golden.

croque madame

8 slices sourdough bread

butter, to spread on bread, plus
2 teaspoons extra to fry eggs

4 thick slices ham

4 slices gruyère or Swiss-style cheese

sea salt

freshly ground black pepper

2½ tablespoons olive oil

4 eggs

to serve

shredded fresh Italian parsley

Spread four slices of bread with butter and top the unbuttered side with ham, cheese, salt and pepper and another slice of bread to make sandwiches. Butter the top of the sandwich, too.

Heat a large non-stick frying pan over a medium heat. Add half the olive oil and swirl to cover the base of the pan. Put two sandwiches in the pan and put another heavy frying pan on top to squash them down. Cook for 1–2 minutes until they are golden underneath, then flip them over, replace the weight and cook for a couple of minutes more. Use the rest of the oil to cook the other two sandwiches. If you have a panini press, this is the time to use it, as an alternative to frying.

While the sandwiches are cooking, melt half the butter in a separate non-stick frying pan over a medium heat. Crack 2 eggs into the pan, being careful not to break the yolks. Cook the eggs for about 2 minutes, or until just set. Wipe out the frying pan and fry the other 2 eggs in the remaining butter in the same way. Place a fried egg on each sandwich and sprinkle with the parsley.

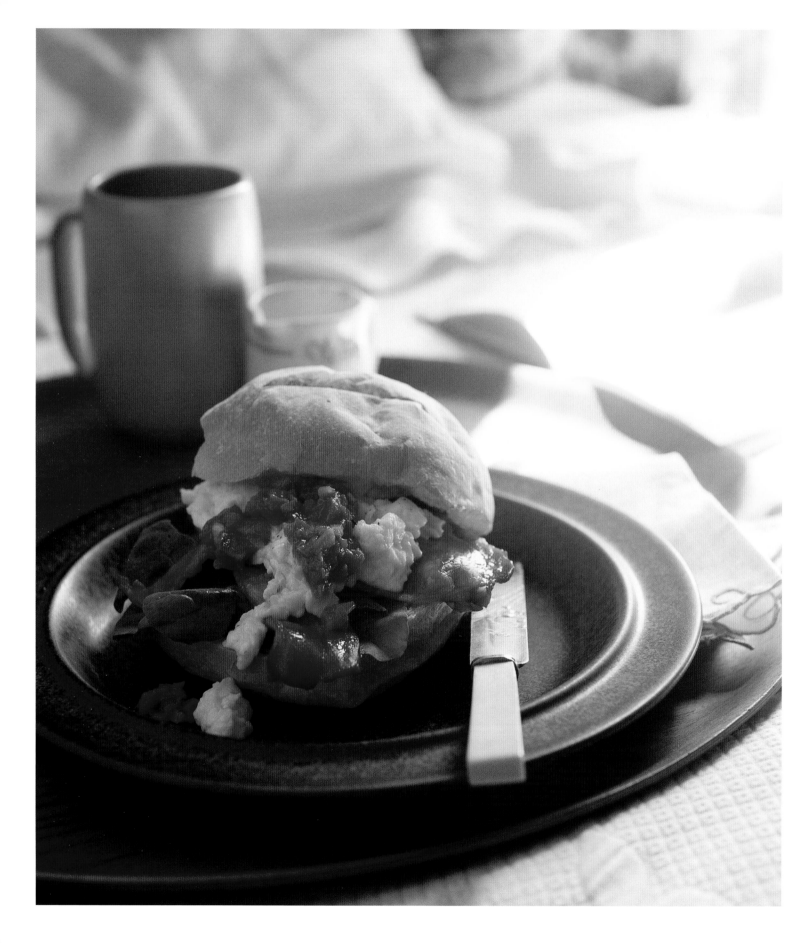

bacon and egg rolls with spicy tomato relish

SERVES 4

4 large slices of bacon, halved

4 eggs

½ cup cream

a pinch of salt

¾ oz butter

to serve

4 soft bread rolls

arugula

spicy tomato relish (see below)

Preheat the oven to 400°F. Line a large baking tray with parchment paper, put the bacon on the tray and bake for 10 minutes, or until crisp. Drain on paper towel.

Meanwhile, whisk together the eggs, cream and salt. Melt the butter in a non-stick frying pan over a high heat, taking care not to let it burn. Pour in the eggs and cook for 20 seconds, or until just set around the edge. With a wooden spoon, gently bring the egg from the outside of the pan to the center — the idea is to "fold" rather than scramble the eggs. Leave them to cook for another 20 seconds, then "fold" again in the same way. When the eggs are just set (remembering that they will continue cooking as they rest) remove from the heat.

Put a couple of pieces of bacon in each roll and top with some egg, arugula and a spoonful of tomato relish.

SPICY TOMATO RELISH

2½ tablespoons olive oil

1 onion, finely chopped

2 garlic cloves, thinly sliced

1 red pepper, seeded and finely diced

1 green pepper, seeded and finely diced

¼ teaspoon cayenne pepper

1 teaspoon paprika

1 fresh red chili, seeded and finely chopped

2 teaspoons tomato paste (concentrated purée)

a pinch of sugar

1 fresh bay leaf

14 oz can chopped tomatoes

Heat the olive oil in a large saucepan over a medium-low heat. Add the onion and cook, stirring occasionally, for 5 minutes or until soft. Add the garlic and cook, stirring, for another 2–3 minutes.

Add the pepper and cook, stirring occasionally, for 10 minutes or until soft. Add the spices, chili and tomato paste and cook, stirring, for 5 minutes. Add the sugar, bay leaf and tomatoes, bring to a low simmer and cook for 40 minutes. Season to taste with salt and pepper before serving.

chocolate-filled french toast

3 eggs

¾ cup milk

4 teaspoons superfine sugar

a pinch of salt

¾ oz unsalted butter

8 slices white bread

3½ oz milk or dark chocolate, chopped

to serve

confectioners sugar

Whisk together the eggs, milk, superfine sugar and salt in a large, shallow dish. Heat the butter in a large non-stick frying pan over medium heat.

Dip two slices of the bread into the egg mixture, turning them over until they are completely coated. Put them in the frying pan and sprinkle each one with a quarter of the chopped chocolate. Soak another two slices of bread in the egg mixture and put on top of the chocolate bread in the pan to make sandwiches. Press lightly with a spatula to seal the edges.

Cook for 3 minutes each side or until golden brown. Remove from the pan and serve immediately or keep warm while you make the other two sandwiches. Serve dusted with confectioners sugar.

blueberry breakfast scones

2 cups all-purpose flour

4 teaspoons superfine sugar

1 tablespoon baking powder

a pinch of salt

3½ oz cold unsalted butter, cubed

2 eggs, lightly beaten

½ cup cream

½ cup blueberries, frozen or fresh, tossed in a little flour

1 egg, whisked with 4 teaspoons milk, for glazing

Preheat the oven to 400°F and line a baking tray with baking paper.

Pulse the flour, sugar, baking powder and salt in a food processor until combined. Add the butter and pulse until it is roughly combined (there will still be lumps of butter). Tip into a bowl and mix in the eggs and cream with a knife. Gently mix in the blueberries with your hands (tossing them in a bit of flour first prevents them all sinking to the bottom of the dough).

Turn the dough onto a lightly floured surface and press into a 6 inch square. Cut into quarters and then cut each quarter in half. Place on the baking tray and brush with the egg and milk glaze. Bake for 15–20 minutes or until golden. Serve warm, with butter if you like.

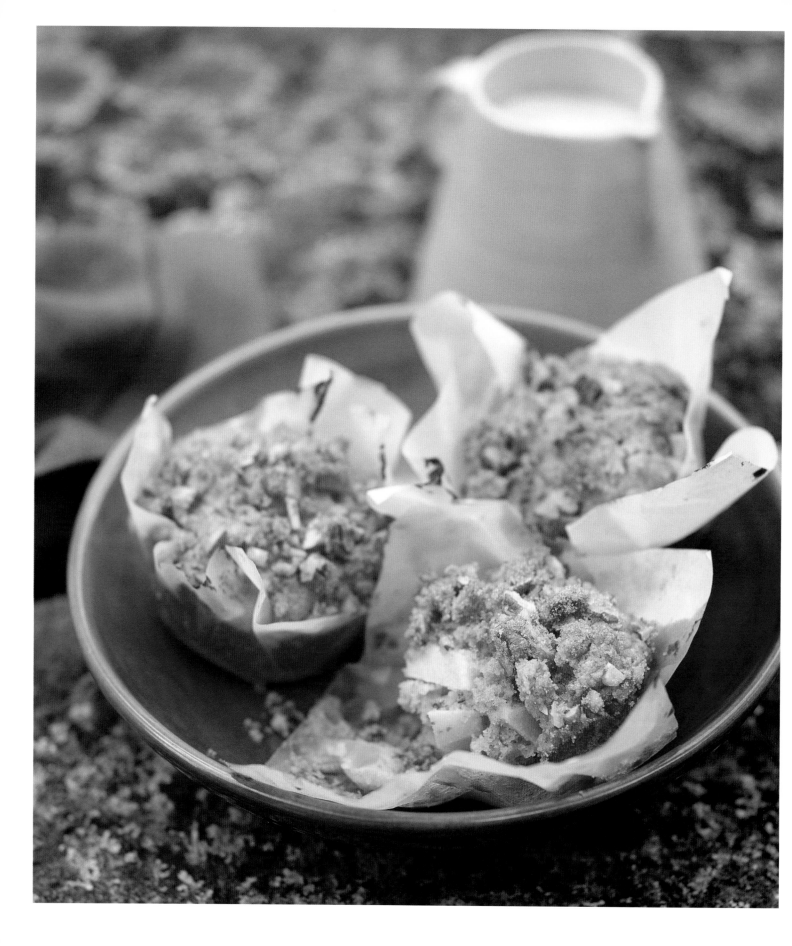

crunchy-top pear muffins

1 cup all-purpose flour
½ cup whole-wheat flour
1 tablespoon baking powder
2 teaspoons ground cinnamon
1 cup rolled oats
¾ cup brown sugar
2 eggs
1 cup plain low-fat yogurt
½ cup grapeseed oil
(or other light-flavored oil)
1 pear, peeled and diced
⅓ cup pecan nuts,
finely chopped

Preheat the oven to 350°F and line six 1 cup muffin holes with baking paper (or just grease well). Sift the flours, baking powder and cinnamon into a large bowl, add the oats and ½ cup of the brown sugar and stir together. Make a well in the center.

Whisk together the eggs, yogurt and oil. Pour into the well in the dry ingredients and stir until just combined. Fold the pear through, being careful not to overmix. Spoon into the muffin pan.

To make the crumble topping, mix the pecans with the remaining brown sugar. Sprinkle over the muffin mixture and then bake for 20–25 minutes until golden brown.

berry hotcakes

1¼ cups frozen mixed berries, thawed

¼ cup superfine sugar

¾ cup all-purpose flour

⅔ cup whole-wheat flour

1¼ teaspoons baking powder

a pinch of salt

3 eggs, separated

1 cup skim milk

½ cup fresh ricotta

a little melted butter, for frying

to serve

maple syrup

Lightly mash the berries with a tablespoon of the sugar and set aside.

Sift the flours, baking powder and salt into a large mixing bowl and add the remaining sugar. In a separate bowl, whisk together the egg yolks and milk. Make a well in the center of the dry ingredients and stir in the egg mixture until just combined. Gently stir in the ricotta.

Beat the egg whites until stiff peaks form. Carefully fold into the batter until just combined. Fold in the berries in two or three strokes to give a marbled effect—do not overmix.

Heat a large frying pan over medium–high heat and brush with a little melted butter. For each hotcake, drop ⅓ cup of the batter into the pan. Cook for 2 minutes, or until bubbles appear on the surface. Turn and cook the other side for 1 minute. Serve with maple syrup.

apple, dried cherry and almond loaf

MAKES 12 SLICES

½ cup old-fashioned oats
10½ fl oz milk
2 cups self-rising flour
1 teaspoon baking powder
4½ oz dried cherries
⅔ cup dried apple, diced
⅓ cup soft brown sugar
1 teaspoon ground cinnamon
¼ cup honey
1 egg, lightly beaten
¼ cup roughly chopped raw almonds,
plus 2½ tablespoons extra

to serve
fresh ricotta cheese
honey

Put the oats in a bowl, pour the milk over them and leave to soak for 30 minutes. Preheat the oven to 350°F. Lightly grease and line a 4 cups capacity loaf pan with parchment paper.

Sift the flour and baking powder into a bowl and stir in the old-fashioned oats, dried fruit, sugar, cinnamon, honey, egg and almonds. Mix together well.

Spoon the mixture into the tin, level the top and sprinkle with the extra almonds. Bake the loaf for 45 minutes, or until it is golden brown on top and cooked through. Leave it to cool a little in the pan before turning out onto a wire rack to cool completely. Toast and serve with ricotta cheese and honey.

lunch

Lunch revives the senses. One of the world's best lunches is a fresh baguette with cheese. In winter, however, lunch to me says soup with fresh herbs and a piece of crunchy bread.

I'm not sure if I should admit this, but when I was a little boy I'd sometimes sneak a day off school when I wasn't really sick. Mum was pretty cool about it. We'd go to a local café and have those open sandwiches, which were huge in late seventies Melbourne. Sandwiches you had to eat with a knife and fork seemed like the height of sophistication and were a far cry from the soggy tomato ones I was more familiar with.

If you're entertaining at lunch, you don't need to serve a lot of different things and, although I'm constantly experimenting with new flavors and methods, there's nothing wrong with finding the things you do really well and sticking with them. The most important thing is to be relaxed when entertaining. If you're relaxed, the food will be better.

spicy tomato and fennel soup

4lb 8 oz vine-ripened tomatoes
6 garlic cloves, peeled
1 small carrot, diced
½ small fennel bulb, finely chopped
¼ cup extra virgin olive oil
2 teaspoons sea salt
freshly ground black pepper

to serve
handful of fresh basil leaves (optional)
extra virgin olive oil
ricotta toast (see below)

Preheat the oven to 400°F. Place the tomatoes, garlic, carrot and fennel in a roasting pan. Drizzle with the olive oil and sprinkle with the salt and pepper. Cover with foil and bake for 1½ hours. Uncover and bake for another 30 minutes, or until the vegetables are well cooked.

Transfer the vegetables to a food processor or blender and blend until combined. What you are looking for is a smoothish mixture with some texture. If you prefer a completely smooth consistency, you can pass the soup through a strainer, but I personally love it with a bit of texture.

Serve in bowls. Top each with basil leaves if you wish and a drizzle of extra virgin olive oil. Serve with ricotta toast.

To make ricotta toast, spread some fresh ricotta cheese on slices of bread, drizzle with olive oil and cook under a hot broiler until golden.

60

rice paper roll

MAKES 20 ROLLS

10½ oz thick rump steaks
7 oz rice vermicelli

marinade
1 fresh lemongrass stalk, white part only, roughly chopped
3 garlic cloves
1 small fresh red chili, seeded
¼ cup fish sauce
4 teaspoons lime juice
2½ tablespoons vegetable oil

to serve
1 oak leaf lettuce, washed and dried
bunch of fresh basil
bunch of fresh mint
2 Lebanese cucumbers, halved lengthways, then thinly sliced on the diagonal
20 large round rice paper wrappers
Vietnamese dipping sauce (below)

Place all the marinade ingredients with ¼ cup water in a food processor or blender and process until smooth. Put the steaks in a bowl and pour the marinade over. Cover with plastic wrap and place in the refrigerator to marinate for 2 hours. Place the rice vermicelli in a bowl and cover with boiling water. Soak for 6–7 minutes, then drain and place on a serving dish.

Place a large frying pan over a high heat until hot. Sear the steaks for 2 minutes on each side, by which time they will be done if you like rare steak. Continue cooking over a medium heat for 1–2 minutes on each side for medium and 2–3 minutes on each side for well done. Remove the steaks and allow to rest for 2 minutes in a warm place. Slice thinly and place on a serving dish.

To serve, arrange the lettuce, basil, mint and cucumber on a large platter and place on the table, alongside the steak, vermicelli, rice paper wrappers and dipping sauce. Place a large bowl of hot water on the table. To wrap the rolls, your guests should first soften the rice paper wrappers in hot water and shake off any excess water. Place the wrapper on a plate, top with a little vermicelli, beef, cucumber, basil and mint in the middle and roll up, tucking in the sides. Place each roll in a lettuce leaf and dip into sauce.

VIETNAMESE DIPPING SAUCE

¼ cup fish sauce
¼ cup lime juice
2½ tablespoons rice vinegar
4 teaspoons superfine sugar
1 garlic clove, finely chopped
1 large fresh red chili, seeded and finely chopped

Place all the ingredients in a bowl and stir until the sugar is dissolved.

If you don't have rice vinegar, just use extra lime juice to taste. What you are looking for is a balance of sweet, salty and sour.

63

crab and asparagus risotto

SERVES 4

6 cups chicken or fish stock
4 teaspoons extra virgin olive oil
1 small onion, finely diced
1 teaspoon sea salt
1¾ oz butter
1½ cups arborio rice
8 asparagus spears, finely sliced
on the diagonal
9 oz cooked fresh crabmeat
grated zest of 1 lemon
¼ cup lemon juice
sea salt, extra, to taste
freshly ground black pepper
fresh chervil sprigs, for garnishing

Pour the stock into a saucepan and bring to the boil. Reduce the heat and keep at simmering point.

Place a large heavy-based saucepan over a medium heat and add the oil, onion, salt and half the butter. Stir until the onion is translucent. Add the rice and stir for 1–2 minutes, until the rice is well coated. Add a cupful of stock at a time, stirring constantly and being sure that each addition of stock is absorbed before you add more.

Continue adding the stock for about 25 minutes. Add the asparagus and continue to add the remaining stock for about another 2 minutes, or until the rice is *al dente* and creamy. Remove the saucepan from the heat, stir in the remaining butter, the crabmeat, lemon zest and juice, and salt and pepper, to taste. Cover the saucepan and leave to sit for 3 minutes to allow the flavors to develop. Stir and divide among four bowls. Top with the chervil sprigs.

Although I've used arborio rice here, you can use other risotto rices such as vialone nano or carnaroli.

zucchini fritters with yogurt sauce

MAKES 18 FRITTERS

1 lb 2 oz zucchini, grated
½ teaspoon sea salt
8 scallions, chopped
4½ oz feta cheese, crumbled
½ cup Italian parsley, chopped
¼ cup fresh mint, chopped
2 eggs, lightly beaten
½ cup all-purpose flour
sea salt, extra, to taste
freshly ground black pepper
¼ cup olive oil, for shallow-frying

to serve
yogurt sauce (see below)
lime wedges

Put the zucchini in a colander, sprinkle with the sea salt, toss lightly and set aside for 30 minutes. Squeeze out the excess liquid from the zucchini and pat dry with paper towels.

Put the zucchini, spring onion, feta, parsley, mint and eggs in a bowl and stir lightly to combine. Stir in the flour, and season with salt and pepper.

Heat the oil in a non-stick frying pan over a medium to high heat. Drop tablespoons of the batter into the hot oil, flattening gently with the back of a spoon. Cook for 2 minutes on each side, or until golden brown. Drain on paper towels and serve with the yogurt sauce and lime wedges.

YOGURT SAUCE

1 garlic clove, finely minced
4 teaspoons extra virgin olive oil
½ cup plain yogurt
2½ tablespoons lemon juice
sea salt
freshly ground black pepper

Put all the ingredients in a bowl and stir to combine.

shrimp and rice vermicelli salad

9 oz rice vermicelli
½ cup soy sauce
¼ cup rice vinegar
1 tablespoon oil mixed with 1 finely sliced
large fresh red chili
2 tablespoons sugar
2 tablespoons peanut oil
1¼ x 1½ inch piece of fresh ginger,
finely julienned
12 cooked shrimp, peeled, deveined, and
sliced in half lengthways
2 Lebanese cucumbers, julienned
4 scallions, finely sliced on the diagonal

to serve
¼ cup fresh cilantro sprigs
¼ cup fresh mint sprigs
lime wedges

Put the rice vermicelli in a bowl and pour in enough boiling water to cover. Soak for 6–7 minutes, then drain and refresh under cold water before draining thoroughly.

Stir the soy sauce, rice vinegar, chili oil, sugar, peanut oil and ginger together in a large bowl until the sugar is dissolved. Add the noodles, shrimp, cucumber and scallions and stir carefully to combine.

Divide among four plates and top with cilantro and mint. Serve with lime wedges.

crispy-skinned salmon with fresh noodle salad and soy dressing

14 oz fresh cilantro egg noodles or other fresh egg noodles

4 salmon fillets, 1 inch thick, skin on

2½ tablespoons oil

sea salt

freshly ground black pepper

1 cucumber, finely julienned

1 cup finely julienned daikon radish

2 scallions, finely sliced on the diagonal

soy dressing (see below)

to serve

lime wedges

Bring a large saucepan of water to a boil over a high heat, add the noodles and blanch for 1 minute. Refresh under cold water.

Heat a frying pan over a high heat for 2 minutes. Brush the salmon fillets with the oil and season liberally with the salt and pepper. Cook the salmon with the skin side down for 2 minutes, then turn over and cook for another 2 minutes. Remove from the pan and allow to rest for 2 minutes. The salmon should be quite rare and the skin crispy.

To assemble the salad, divide the noodles among four plates. Arrange the cucumber and daikon over the noodles and sprinkle with scallion. Put a salmon fillet on each plate and drizzle with soy dressing. Serve with lime wedges.

2 teaspoons sesame oil

½ cup soy sauce

2 tablespoons balsamic vinegar

2½ tablespoons superfine sugar

¼ cup lime juice

2 small fresh red chilies, finely chopped (optional)

SOY DRESSING

Stir all the dressing ingredients together in a bowl until the sugar is dissolved.

spiced zucchini soup

2 small white onions, or 1 large white
onion, roughly chopped
4 teaspoons olive oil
a pinch of sea salt
4 teaspoons curry powder
2 lb 4 oz zucchini, sliced
6 cups vegetable or chicken stock
freshly ground black pepper
¼ cup short-grain rice

to serve
plain yogurt
1 zucchini, shaved into thin ribbons
and lightly blanched

Place the onion, olive oil and salt in a large saucepan over a medium to high heat and cook for 5 minutes, or until the onion is translucent. Add the curry powder and cook for 2 minutes. Add the zucchini, stock, pepper and rice and bring to a boil. Reduce the heat to low and cook for another 20 minutes.

Blend the soup in a blender or food processor until smooth. Serve immediately with a dollop of yogurt and garnish with zucchini ribbons.

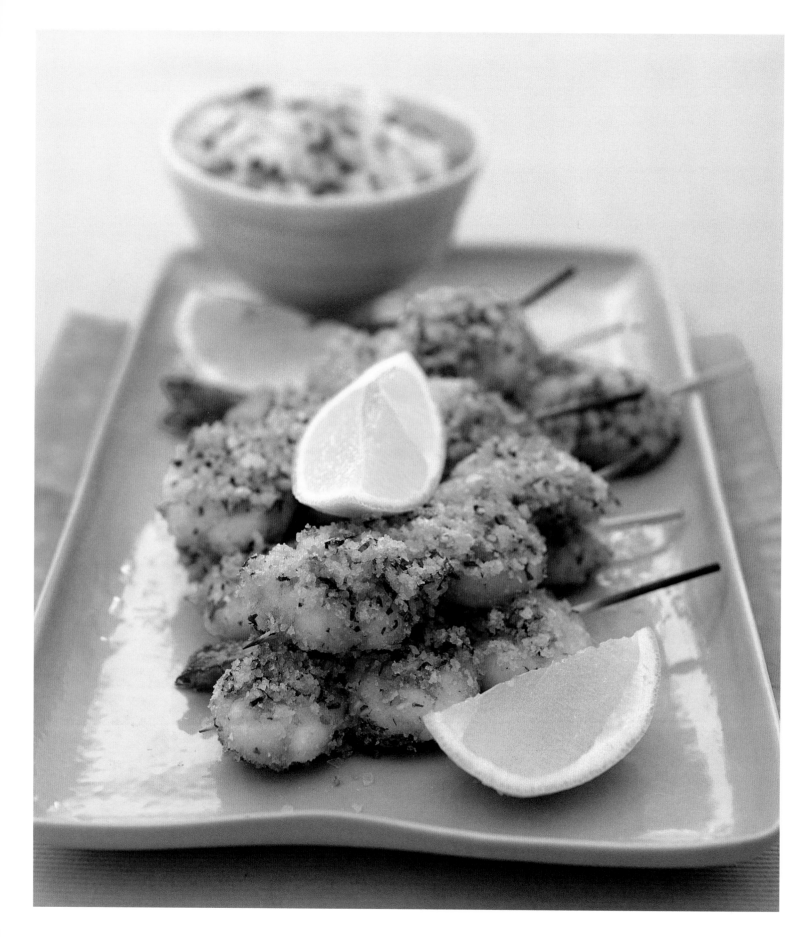

shrimp skewers with rice salad

3 thick slices sourdough or wholegrain bread, crusts removed

⅓ cup extra virgin olive oil

24 medium raw shrimp, peeled and deveined

2 garlic cloves, crushed

¼ cup fresh Italian parsley, finely chopped

finely grated zest of 1 lemon

1 teaspoon sea salt

freshly ground black pepper

to serve

lemon wedges

rice salad (see below)

Soak eight wooden skewers in water for 30 minutes to stop them from burning during cooking. Preheat the oven to 400°F. Place the bread on a baking sheet and toast for 20 minutes, or until lightly golden. Remove from the oven and leave to cool. Crumble the toasted bread with your hands or process in a food processor until breadcrumbs form.

Place the olive oil and shrimp in a large bowl and toss to combine. Add the remaining ingredients and stir thoroughly so that each shrimp is evenly coated with breadcrumbs. Cover with plastic wrap and refrigerate for 30 minutes. Preheat the broiler to high. Thread 3 shrimp on each skewer, curling and skewering the tails to maintain a round shape.

Place on a baking sheet and cook for 2 minutes each side, or until golden. Serve with lemon wedges and the rice salad.

RICE SALAD

¼ cup olive oil

2½ tablespoons lemon juice

a pinch of sea salt

freshly ground black pepper

4 cups cooked short-grain rice

4 teaspoons lemon zest

½ red onion, finely diced

⅓ cup fresh Italian parsley, roughly chopped

2 celery stalks, finely diced

⅓ cup green olives, pitted and sliced

Combine the oil, lemon juice, salt and pepper in a serving bowl. Add the remaining ingredients and toss until well combined.

This rice salad can be made ahead of time and refrigerated. If cooking the rice ahead of time, cool down quickly and refrigerate until required. Stand at room temperature for 15 minutes before serving.

vietnamese chicken salad

SERVES 4

3 x 7 oz chicken breasts, skin on
2½ tablespoons vegetable oil
a pinch of sea salt
pepper (I like white pepper in this salad,
but use black if that is all you have)
1 cup bean sprouts
1 cup fresh Vietnamese mint leaves
1 cup fresh Asian basil leaves,
or fresh basil leaves
4 cups Chinese cabbage,
finely shredded
Vietnamese dressing (see below)
1 cup pickled carrot (see below), or raw
carrot, peeled and finely julienned

Preheat the oven to 425°F. Heat a frying pan over a high heat, and while the pan is heating, brush the chicken with the oil and season with salt and pepper.

Place the chicken skin-side down and sear for 2 minutes, turn and sear for another minute. Put the chicken on a baking tray and cook in the oven for 8–10 minutes. Leave to rest for 20 minutes. Shred the chicken into thin strips with your hands and place in a large bowl. Add the remaining ingredients and toss to combine.

¼ cup lime juice
¼ cup fish sauce
2½ tablespoons rice vinegar
4 teaspoons superfine sugar
2 garlic cloves, very finely chopped
3 red Asian shallots, or ½ red onion,
finely sliced
2 small fresh red chilies, very finely
chopped (seeds removed, if you don't
like the heat)

VIETNAMESE DRESSING

Place all the ingredients in a small bowl and stir until the sugar is dissolved.

9 oz carrots, peeled and finely julienned
1 teaspoon sea salt
2½ tablespoons rice vinegar
4 teaspoons superfine sugar

PICKLED CARROT

Place the carrots in a colander, sprinkle with the salt and toss to combine. Leave for 20 minutes. While the carrot is resting, place ¾ cup water with the vinegar and sugar in a small saucepan over a medium heat and bring to a boil. Remove from the heat and cool. Rinse the carrot, squeezing out any excess water, and place in a bowl. Pour over the pickling liquid and stand for 1 hour. Strain before serving.

76

burger with hummus and potato wedges

SERVES 4

4 good-quality hamburger buns or rolls

1 lb 2 oz lean ground beef

1 red onion, grated

a pinch of sea salt

freshly ground black pepper

¼ cup olive oil

9 oz cherry tomatoes, sliced

½ teaspoon sumac

1 small white salad onion, cut into thin wedges

¼ cup fresh Italian parsley, shredded

4 teaspoons lemon juice

hummus (see below)

potato wedges (see below)

Cut the buns horizontally into halves. Put the ground beef, onion, salt and pepper in a bowl and combine well with your hands. Form into four patties, making them slightly larger than the buns because they will shrink during cooking.

Heat 2 tablespoons of the oil in a large non-stick frying pan over a medium to high heat, add the hamburger patties and, because the patties tend to puff up, make a small dip in the center of each with the back of a spoon. Cook for 4 minutes on each side, or until done to your liking.

Make the salad by tossing the cherry tomatoes, sumac, onion and parsley together with the remaining olive oil and the lemon juice. While the burgers are cooking, toast the buns with the cut side up. Spread hummus on the toasted sides, then top with a patty, salad and the bun tops. Serve with potato wedges.

HUMMUS

14 oz canned chickpeas, drained

1 garlic clove

2½ tablespoons lemon juice

sea salt

freshly ground black pepper

Process the chickpeas, garlic and lemon juice in a food processor with ¼ cup of water until the hummus is smooth. Season, to taste, with salt and pepper.

POTATO WEDGES

2 tablespoons vegetable oil

5 garlic cloves, unpeeled and crushed with the side of a knife

2 tablespoons lime juice

2 teaspoons Tabasco sauce

1 lb potatoes, unpeeled, scrubbed, dried and cut into wedges

freshly ground black pepper

sea salt

Preheat the oven to 400°F. Put the oil, garlic, lime juice and Tabasco sauce in a large bowl and whisk to combine. Add the potatoes and pepper and stir until the potatoes are coated. Transfer to a baking dish, spreading the potatoes evenly over the dish with the rounded side down. Bake for 45 minutes, or until crispy. Sprinkle with sea salt and serve.

warm tomato and ricotta pasta salad

SERVES 4

1 lb 2 oz cherry tomatoes,
cut in half
½ cup extra virgin olive oil
¼ cup red wine vinegar
½ teaspoon superfine sugar
1 teaspoon sea salt
freshly ground black pepper
4 thick slices whole wheat or
sourdough bread
1 garlic clove, sliced in half
1 lb 2 oz rigatoni
1 cup fresh basil leaves, finely shredded
1 cup fresh ricotta cheese

Preheat the oven to 400°F. Place the tomatoes, ⅓ cup olive oil, the vinegar and sugar in a large bowl and stir to combine. Season with the salt and pepper. Cover and leave to marinate while you prepare the rest of the dish.

Rub the bread on both sides with the cut side of the garlic. Brush with the remaining olive oil and sprinkle with salt. Put the bread on a baking tray and place in the oven. Cook for 20 minutes, or until crisp. Remove from the oven and crumble into coarse breadcrumbs with your hands. Set aside.

Cook the pasta in a large saucepan of rapidly boiling salted water until *al dente*. Drain well, then add to the tomatoes. Add the basil and toss to combine.

Divide the pasta between four serving plates, or put it on one large serving dish, crumble over the ricotta cheese and sprinkle with the breadcrumbs.

chorizo, potato and red pepper frittata

2 tablespoons olive oil
1 chorizo sausage, sliced
1 red-skinned potato, diced
1 small onion, diced
1 red pepper, diced
10 eggs
2½ tablespoons fresh Italian parsley, chopped
2½ tablespoons finely grated parmesan cheese

Heat 2 teaspoons olive oil in a 8 inch frying pan over medium-high heat and cook the chorizo, stirring occasionally, for 5–6 minutes, or until crisp. Drain on paper towel.

Turn the heat to medium, add the remaining oil, the potato and onion to the pan and cook, stirring occasionally, for 5 minutes, or until the onion is soft. Add the pepper and cook for 5 minutes before returning the chorizo to the pan. Preheat your broiler to hot.

Whisk the eggs and pour into the pan. Reduce the heat to low, cover the pan and cook until the eggs have almost set. Sprinkle with parsley and parmesan cheese and then put the pan under the broiler for 3–4 minutes until the frittata is golden and puffed.

spaghettini with lemon, prosciutto and chili

SERVES 4

¼ cup lemon juice

¼ cup extra virgin olive oil

2 small fresh red chilies, seeded and finely chopped

a pinch of sea salt

freshly ground black pepper

12 slices prosciutto, cut into thin strips

4 teaspoons grated lemon zest

9 oz arugula, shredded

14 oz good-quality dried thin spaghettini

Whisk the lemon juice, olive oil, chili, salt and pepper in a bowl to blend.

Put the prosciutto, lemon zest and the arugula in a bowl and toss to combine.

Bring a large saucepan of salted water to a boil. Add the spaghettini and cook until *al dente*. Drain and add to the prosciutto and arugula. Pour the dressing over and toss to combine.

Transfer to a large serving dish or divide among four bowls.

Remember, with simple recipes such as this one, you can throw in any of your favorite ingredients.

citrus risotto with garlic chili shrimp

SERVES 4

6 cups chicken stock
4 teaspoons olive oil
1 small onion, finely diced
1 teaspoon sea salt
1¾ oz butter
1½ cups arborio rice
finely grated zest of 1 lemon
4 teaspoons lemon juice
freshly ground black pepper
2 small fresh red chilies
2 garlic cloves
2½ tablespoons olive oil, extra
20 raw shrimp, peeled and deveined, with tails intact

to serve
¼ cup Italian parsley, roughly chopped
lemon wedges

Place the stock in a large saucepan and bring to a boil over a high heat. Reduce the heat and keep at simmering point. Place a large heavy-based saucepan over a medium heat and add the olive oil, onion, salt and half of the butter. Stir until the onion is translucent. Add the rice and stir for 1–2 minutes, or until the rice is well coated.

Gradually add the simmering stock, a cupful at a time, stirring constantly and making sure the stock is absorbed before you add more. This should take 20 minutes and the rice should be *al dente* and creamy. Remove the saucepan from the heat, then stir in the remaining butter, lemon zest, lemon juice and pepper to taste. Cover the saucepan and leave to sit for 3 minutes for the flavors to develop.

Meanwhile, pound the chili and garlic in a mortar and pestle. Place the extra olive oil in a frying pan over a high heat and heat until hot. Season the shrimp with salt and pepper. Cook for 2 minutes, shaking the pan, until the shrimp are just opaque then add the chili and garlic and cook for 1 minute. Remove from the heat and set aside.

Stir risotto and divide between four bowls. Toss the shrimp with the parsley then place on top of the risotto. Serve with lemon wedges.

briget's onion and feta cheese tart

SERVES 6

2½ tablespoons olive oil

2 lb 4 oz onions, finely sliced

4 teaspoons soft brown sugar

2½ tablespoons balsamic vinegar

I teaspoon sea salt

freshly ground black pepper

13 oz block puff pastry

½ cup finely grated parmesan cheese

I cup feta cheese, crumbled

2½ tablespoons oregano leaves

Place the olive oil and onion in a saucepan over a medium heat and cook for 20 minutes, stirring occasionally. Add the sugar, balsamic vinegar, salt and pepper. Cook for another 5 minutes, or until the onion is soft and caramelized. Remove from the heat and set aside to cool.

Meanwhile, preheat the oven to 425°F. Roll out the pastry to an 8 × 16 inch rectangle on a lightly floured surface. Trim the edges with a sharp knife and place on a baking tray lined with parchment paper. Score a ½ inch border around the edge of the pastry, taking care not to cut all the way through to the bottom. Prick pastry with a fork and sprinkle the parmesan cheese within the scored edges.

Place the onion on top of the parmesan. Bake in the oven for 20–25 minutes, or until the pastry is puffed and golden brown. Remove from the oven and sprinkle with the feta cheese and oregano leaves.

tagliatelle with chicken and green beans

2 x 7 oz chicken breasts, thinly sliced

2½ tablespoons extra virgin olive oil

3 garlic cloves, sliced

sea salt

freshly ground black pepper

13 oz tagliatelle (I like to use fresh spinach tagliatelle, but plain fresh pasta will be just as delicious)

2½ tablespoons olive oil

7 oz baby green beans, topped (not tailed) and sliced from end to end, on the diagonal

½ cup chicken stock

good-quality parmesan cheese, grated

¼ cup fresh basil leaves

Place the chicken, extra virgin olive oil and garlic in a bowl and stir to combine. Season with the salt and pepper. Cook the pasta in a large saucepan of rapidly boiling salted water until *al dente* and drain well.

Meanwhile, when the pasta is almost ready, place a large frying pan over a high heat until hot. Add the extra olive oil and heat for 5 seconds. Add the chicken with the marinade and sear quickly for 30 seconds. Add the beans and reduce the heat to medium. Cook for another 2 minutes, stirring occasionally. Return the heat to high, add the stock and simmer for 30 seconds. Add the pasta and toss to combine.

Divide the pasta evenly between four bowls and top with the freshly grated parmesan cheese and basil.

barbecued
duck salad

1 Chinese roast duck
6 scallions, sliced on the diagonal
2 Lebanese cucumbers, julienned
1 cup fresh cilantro leaves
1 large fresh red chili, thinly sliced

to serve
dressing (see below)
steamed rice

Pull the skin and meat from the duck with your fingers, roughly shredding both. Place the duck, scallions, cucumber, cilantro and chili in a bowl and toss to combine. Drizzle over the dressing just before serving with steamed rice, or serve alongside.

DRESSING

3½ tablespoons hoisin sauce
2½ tablespoons soy sauce
4 teaspoons balsamic vinegar
2 teaspoons sesame oil

Place all the ingredients in a bowl and stir to combine.

I buy my roast ducks in Chinatown at a Chinese barbecue shop.

94

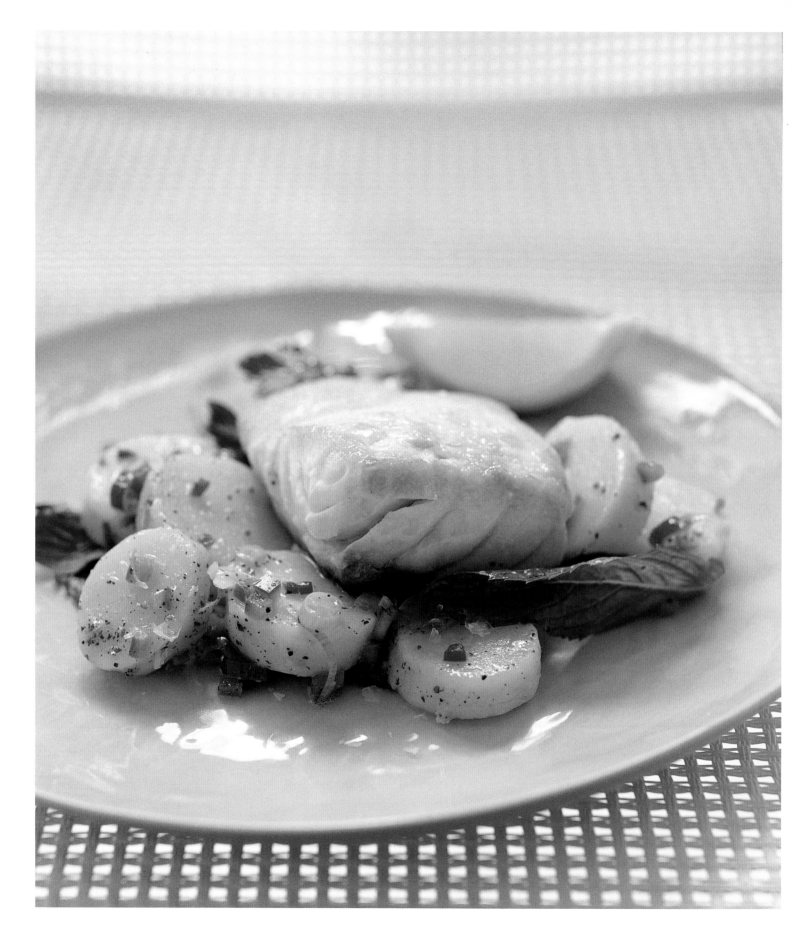

pan-fried fish with lemon potato salad

SERVES 4

olive oil, for greasing the pan

4 x 7 oz firm white fish fillets, such as snapper, skin removed

to serve

lemon wedges

mint leaves

lemon potato salad (see below)

Heat a little oil in a large non-stick frying pan over a medium to high heat until hot. Add the fish and cook for 3 minutes. Turn and cook on the other side for 2–3 minutes, or until the fish is opaque and just cooked. Garnish with mint leaves and serve with lemon wedges and the lemon potato salad.

1 lb 10 oz waxy potatoes, such as kipfler, peeled and sliced

1 teaspoon sea salt

$1/3$ cup extra virgin olive oil

$1/2$ cup lemon juice

1 teaspoon sumac (optional)

sea salt, extra

freshly ground black pepper

1 small green pepper, finely diced

2 large fresh red chilies, seeded and finely diced

$1/4$ cup fresh mint, chopped

$1\frac{1}{2}$ cups fresh Italian parsley, thinly sliced

6 scallions, thinly sliced

LEMON POTATO SALAD

Bring a large saucepan of water to a boil over a high heat. Add the potatoes and salt, reduce the heat to medium and simmer for about 8–10 minutes until the potatoes are tender when pierced with a knife. Remember to undercook the potatoes a little, because they will continue cooking when removed from the water.

Place the olive oil, lemon juice and sumac in a bowl and stir to combine. Season with salt and pepper. Pour half the dressing over the hot potatoes and stir gently. Leave to cool.

Add the pepper, chili, mint, parsley, scallions and remaining dressing and stir gently.

A nice alternative is to make a simple herb crust by mixing chopped parsley and cilantro together with chili, lemon zest, salt, pepper and olive oil. Press firmly on the fish, refrigerate for 30 minutes then cook as above.

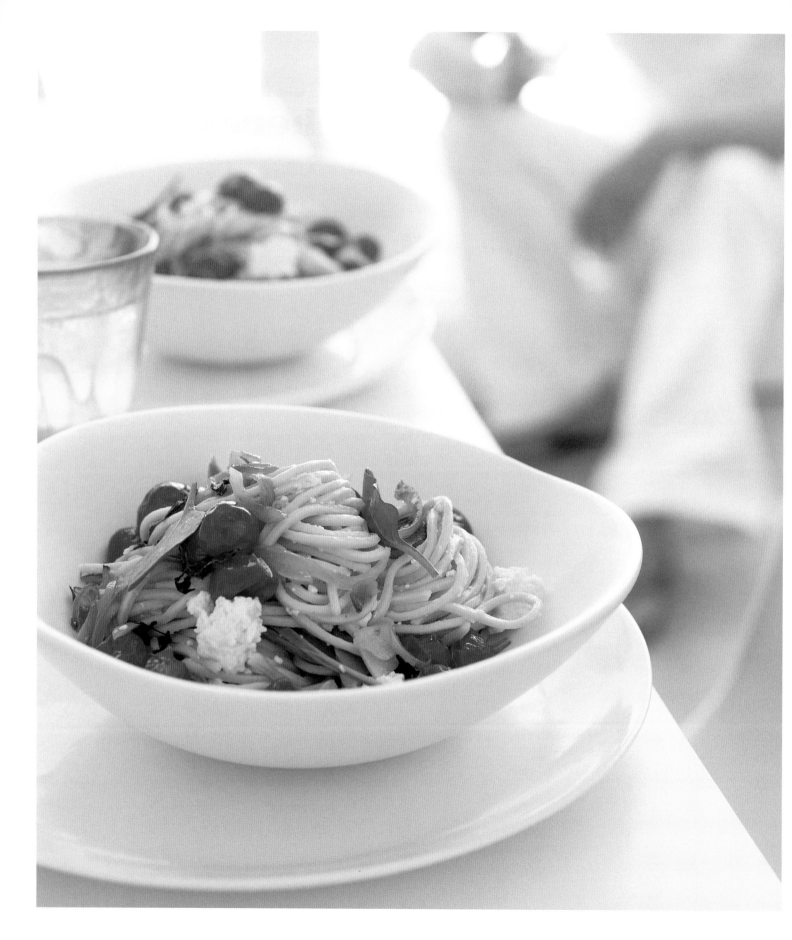

spaghetti with cherry tomatoes, ricotta, spinach and pecorino

5 cups cherry tomatoes
4 garlic cloves, sliced
1 red onion, thinly sliced
small handful of fresh oregano
3½ fl oz extra virgin olive oil
1 lb 2 oz fresh spaghetti
1¾ oz baby English spinach leaves
7 oz fresh ricotta cheese
freshly ground black pepper

to serve
2½ oz pecorino cheese, grated

Preheat the oven to 350°F. Put the tomatoes, garlic, onion and oregano on a baking tray and drizzle with the oil. Roast for 20–25 minutes or until wilted.

Cook the pasta in a large saucepan of boiling salted water until *al dente*. Drain and toss with the tomato mixture, spinach and half of the ricotta. Divide among serving bowls and top with the remaining ricotta cheese and some freshly ground pepper. Serve with the grated pecorino cheese.

I really like to use pecorino sometimes, rather than the more obvious parmesan. Pecorino is an Italian sheep's milk cheese.

99

penne with eggplant and chili

SERVES 4

1 large eggplant, sliced

⅓ cup olive oil

sea salt

4 garlic cloves, thinly sliced

2 large fresh red chilies, thinly sliced

2 x 14 oz cans chopped tomatoes

freshly ground black pepper

1 lb 2 oz penne

small handful of fresh Italian parsley, chopped

Preheat the broiler. Arrange the eggplant on a baking tray, brush liberally with half of the oil and sprinkle with salt on both sides. Grill for 3–6 minutes on each side or until golden brown and cooked. When eggplant is cool enough, cut into small cubes.

Meanwhile, place a frying pan over medium heat. Add the rest of the oil and sauté the garlic, chili and a little salt for 1 minute. Add the tomatoes and pepper and simmer for 10–15 minutes. Gently fold through the eggplant.

Meanwhile, cook the pasta in a large saucepan of boiling salted water until *al dente*. Drain well and toss with the sauce and parsley.

spicy pumpkin soup

4 teaspoons olive oil

1 red onion, sliced

1 inch piece of fresh ginger, sliced

2 teaspoons Thai red curry paste

3 lb 8 oz butternut squash, peeled, seeded and cubed

⅔ cup coconut milk

4 teaspoons fish sauce

4 teaspoons lime juice

1–2 teaspoons sugar, or to taste

to serve

small handful of fresh cilantro leaves, shredded

Place a large saucepan over medium heat. Add the olive oil, onion, ginger and curry paste and cook for 1 minute until fragrant. Add the squash and stir to coat with the paste. Add 4 cups of water and bring to a boil. Reduce the heat and simmer for 30 minutes or until the squash is tender.

Transfer to a blender and mix until smooth. Return to the pan, stir in the coconut milk and season with the fish sauce, lime juice and sugar. Heat through gently before serving. Top with the cilantro leaves.

Soup is always good to make in bulk because it's so easy to freeze — just don't add the cilantro until after you've reheated or it will discolor.

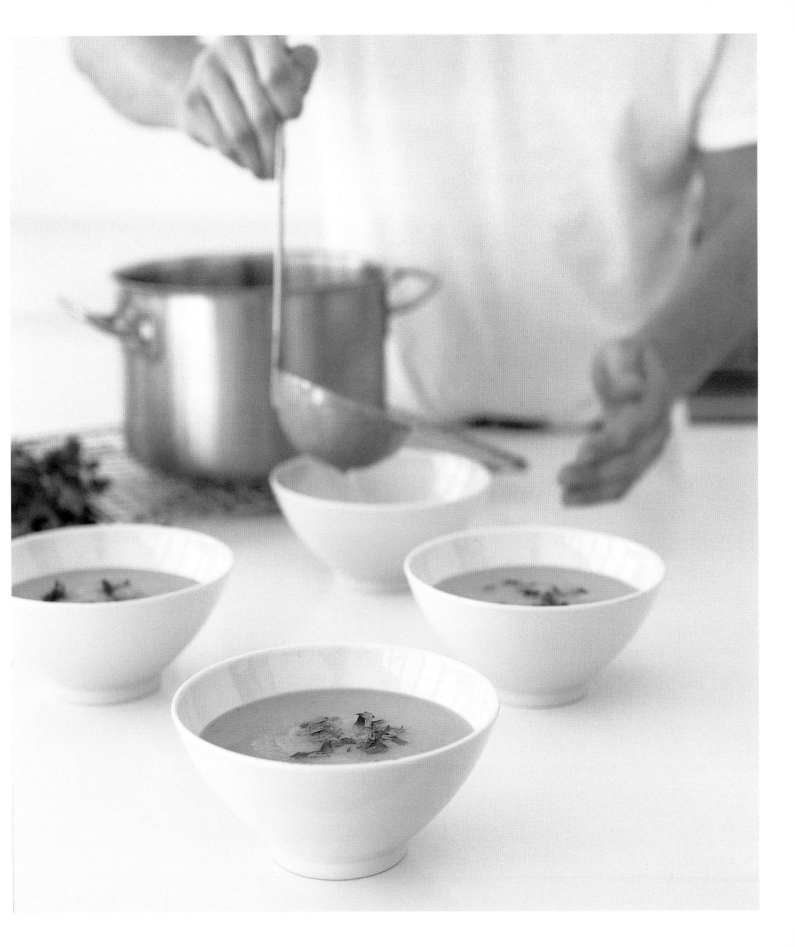

haloumi open sandwich

4 teaspoons olive oil
8 x ½ inch thick slices haloumi cheese
½ lemon
4 slices sourdough bread
⅓ cup hummus
1 Lebanese cucumber, cut into
long wedges
arugula leaves
1 red pepper, roasted, peeled and
cut into quarters
freshly ground black pepper

Heat the olive oil in a large non-stick frying pan over high heat. Add the haloumi and cook for 2 minutes on each side, or until golden brown. Remove from the pan and squeeze with a little lemon juice.

Toast the sourdough and spread with hummus. Top each slice with some cucumber, arugula, roasted pepper and haloumi. Season generously with black pepper.

chickpea stew with tomatoes and green chili

2½ tablespoons olive oil

1 red onion, thinly sliced

3 garlic cloves, thinly sliced

2 teaspoons fresh ginger, grated

1 or 2 fresh green chilies, to taste, seeded
and finely chopped

1 teaspoon sea salt

2 x 14 oz cans chickpeas, rinsed

1 teaspoon ground cumin

½ teaspoon turmeric (optional)

freshly ground black pepper

1 lb 2 oz cherry tomatoes, halved

2¼ cups baby English spinach leaves

to serve

plain yogurt

Heat a large deep frying pan over a medium to high heat. Add the oil, onion, garlic, ginger, chili and salt. Cook, stirring, for 5 minutes, or until the onions are soft. Add the chickpeas, ⅓ cup water, cumin, turmeric, if using, and pepper and cook for 5 minutes, or until the water evaporates. Add the tomatoes and cook for another 2 minutes to soften. Remove from the heat and taste for seasoning. Stir through the spinach and top with yogurt.

I like to serve this dish with pita crisps — just break up pieces of pita bread, drizzle with olive oil, sea salt, black pepper and paprika and bake for 10–12 minutes in a moderate oven until crisp.

L.A. burger with sweet potato fries

1 lb 2 oz ground pork

½ onion, grated

½ teaspoon fennel seeds, lightly toasted and crushed

½ cup fresh white breadcrumbs

1 egg, lightly beaten

4 teaspoons fresh Italian parsley, chopped

sea salt

freshly ground black pepper

to serve

hamburger buns

arugula leaves

roasted red pepper

1 red onion, thinly sliced

sweet potato fries (see below)

Put the pork, onion, fennel, breadcrumbs, egg and parsley in a large mixing bowl. Season well with salt and pepper and then use your hands to mix everything together thoroughly. Shape the mixture into four patties, then cover and leave in the fridge for 30 minutes.

Heat a frying pan over high heat. Add the patties and cook for 4–5 minutes on each side until browned and cooked through.

Place the patties in hamburger buns and top with arugula, roasted pepper and a few slices of red onion. Serve with sweet potato fries.

SWEET POTATO FRIES

2 lb 4 oz sweet potatoes, peeled and cut into strips

2½ tablespoons olive oil

2 teaspoons paprika

¼ teaspoon cayenne pepper

sea salt

Preheat the oven to 450°F. Toss the sweet potato with the olive oil, paprika, cayenne pepper and sea salt. Scatter them in a single layer on a large baking tray and bake for 30 minutes, turning occasionally, until the fries are golden brown.

salmon tartine

½ cup whole green olives, flesh
sliced from the pit
1 lemon, peel and pith removed, cut into
segments
4 teaspoons small salted capers, rinsed
large handful of fresh Italian parsley
8 slices sourdough bread
⅔ cup fresh ricotta cheese
7 oz smoked salmon

Gently toss together the olives, lemon segments, capers and parsley. Toast the sourdough bread until golden. Spread the bread with ricotta and top with smoked salmon. Arrange two slices on each plate and top with some of the olive mixture. Serve immediately.

vegetable soup

1 oz butter

1 large leek, white part only, thinly sliced

2 celery stalks, diced

2 large red-skinned potatoes, diced

1 turnip, peeled and diced

6 cups vegetable stock

sea salt

freshly ground black pepper

½ cup small pasta (such as macaroni)

1 large zucchini, diced

1 cup green beans, topped and
cut into short lengths

1 cup fresh peas

Melt the butter in a large saucepan over medium heat. Add the leek, celery, potato and turnip and cook, stirring frequently, for 5 minutes. Add the vegetable stock, salt and pepper and bring to a boil. Lower the heat and add the remaining ingredients. Simmer gently for 8 minutes until the pasta is cooked and the vegetables are just tender. Ladle into bowls and top with lots of freshly ground black pepper.

roast beef sandwiches with olive caper relish

SERVES 8 WITH LEFTOVERS

3 lb 5 oz piece of beef topside
olive oil, to drizzle
sea salt
freshly ground black pepper

to serve
sourdough bread, or your favorite sandwich bread
arugula leaves
olive caper relish (see below)

Preheat the oven to 425°F. Put the beef on a large baking pan, drizzle with olive oil and season with the salt and pepper. Roast for 15 minutes, or until browned.

Reduce the oven temperature to 400°F and roast the beef for a further 45 minutes (it will be medium-rare). Remove from the oven, cover loosely with foil and set aside to rest for 30 minutes. Thinly slice the beef and use to make sandwiches with the bread, arugula and olive caper relish.

1 cup pitted green olives
4 teaspoons small salted capers, rinsed
2½ tablespoons fresh Italian parsley, chopped
2 teaspoons grated lemon zest
¼ cup extra virgin olive oil
freshly ground black pepper

OLIVE CAPER RELISH

Put the olives, capers, parsley and lemon zest in a food processor and process until finely chopped. Add the olive oil and process until the relish has a coarse pesto-like consistency. Season with the pepper.

poached salmon and orzo salad

SERVES 4 TO 6

4 teaspoons sea salt

½ teaspoon white peppercorns

1 fresh bay leaf

14 oz salmon fillets, skin removed

7 oz orzo

½ cup peas (frozen are fine)

grated zest and juice of 1 lemon

1¼ cups baby spinach leaves

2½ tablespoons Italian parsley, chopped

2 teaspoons fresh dill, chopped

4 teaspoons extra virgin olive oil

a large pinch of superfine sugar

sea salt

freshly ground black pepper

Put the salt, peppercorns and bay leaf in a large, deep frying pan with 3 cups of water and bring to a boil. Simmer for 5 minutes, then remove from the heat. Add the salmon, cover and leave for 15 minutes. Lift the fish carefully out of the stock. When cool enough to handle, flake the fish into pieces, picking out any bones.

Cook the orzo in a large saucepan of boiling salted water until *al dente*, adding the peas and lemon zest for the last 2 minutes of cooking. Rinse under cold running water and drain well.

Put the orzo , salmon, spinach, parsley and dill in a large bowl. Whisk together the lemon juice, olive oil and sugar to make a dressing. Add the dressing to the salad and toss gently. Season with salt and pepper.

spaghetti with asparagus, mint and chili

SERVES 4

14 oz spaghetti

$1/3$ cup extra virgin olive oil

3 garlic cloves, thinly sliced

1 large fresh red chili, seeded and thinly sliced

2 bunches of asparagus (about 14 oz), thinly sliced

handful of fresh mint leaves

sea salt

freshly ground black pepper

to serve

grated parmesan cheese

Cook the spaghetti in a large saucepan of boiling salted water until *al dente*. Reserve half a cupful of the cooking liquid before draining the pasta.

Meanwhile, heat the olive oil in a large, deep frying pan over medium heat. Add the garlic and chili and cook, stirring, for 30 seconds. Add the asparagus and continue to cook, stirring, for 1–2 minutes or until it is bright green and just tender. Add the pasta cooking liquid and simmer for 30 seconds.

Add the hot pasta and mint leaves to the asparagus and toss together. Season and serve immediately with the grated parmesan cheese.

pork, veal and pistachio sausage rolls

4 teaspoons olive oil

1 large onion, finely chopped

2 garlic cloves, crushed

2 teaspoons ground cumin

1 teaspoon ground coriander

1 lb 2 oz ground veal

1 lb 2 oz ground pork

½ cup roughly chopped pistachio nuts

1 egg

sea salt

freshly ground black pepper

4 sheets puff pastry

2 egg yolks

2½ tablespoons milk

sesame seeds, to sprinkle

Preheat the oven to 400°F and line a large baking tray with parchment paper.

Heat the olive oil in a frying pan over a medium heat. Add the onion and cook, stirring occasionally, for 5–6 minutes until softened. Add the garlic and spices and cook, stirring, for another minute.

Set aside to cool, then tip into a large bowl. Add the veal, pork, pistachios and egg and mix with your hands until thoroughly combined. Season with sea salt and freshly ground black pepper.

Cut each pastry sheet in half, so you have eight pieces. Working with one piece of pastry at a time, spread an eighth of the filling down the middle of the pastry in a log shape.

Mix together the egg yolks and milk and brush around the outside edges of each piece of pastry. Roll up and cut each roll into two pieces. Place on the baking tray with the sealed edges underneath.

Brush the tops of the sausage rolls with the egg wash and sprinkle with sesame seeds. Bake for 25–30 minutes or until golden brown and cooked through.

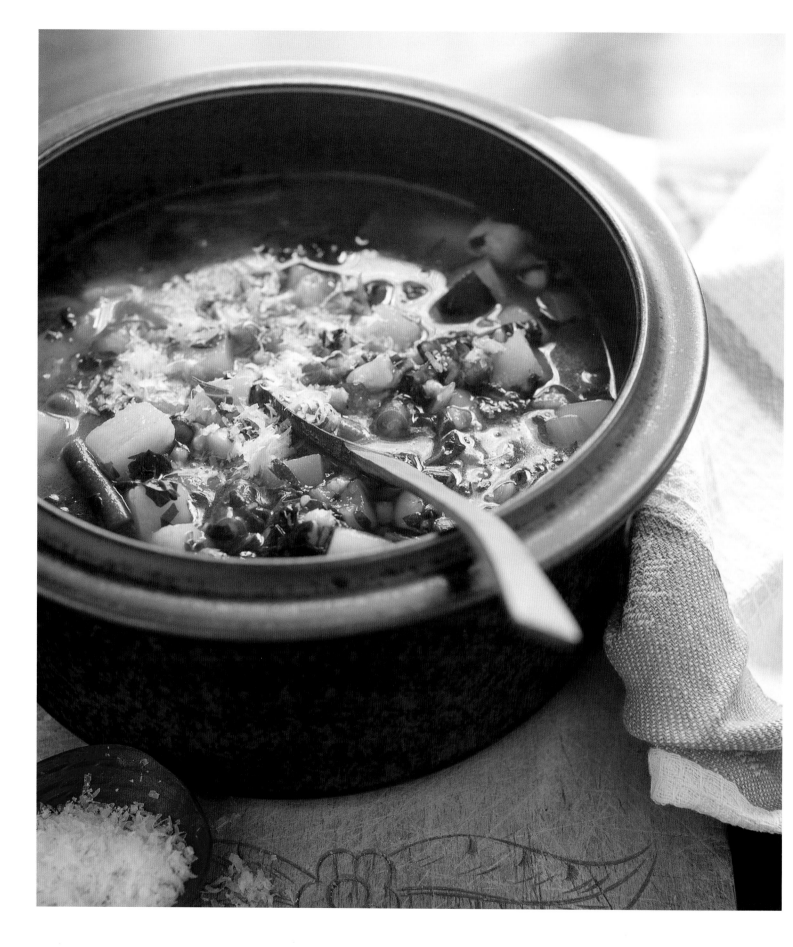

barley, bean and vegetable soup

½ cup barley
2½ tablespoons olive oil
1 onion, diced
2 zucchini, diced
2 red-skinned potatoes, peeled and diced
2 garlic cloves, crushed
1 lb 9 oz swiss chard, finely shredded
4 cups chicken or vegetable stock
14 oz can cannellini beans, rinsed
7 oz green beans, topped and cut into short lengths
½ cup peas (fresh or frozen)
sea salt
freshly ground black pepper

to serve
parmesan cheese

Put barley in a large saucepan, cover with cold water and bring to a boil. Reduce the heat and simmer for 45 minutes, or until barley is tender. Rinse under cold running water, drain well and set aside.

Heat the olive oil in a large heavy-based saucepan over medium heat. Add the onion and cook, stirring occasionally, for 5 minutes. Add the zucchini, potato, garlic and swiss chard and cook, stirring occasionally, for 5 minutes more until the swiss chard has wilted.

Add the stock and 4 cups of water and bring to a boil. Reduce the heat to low and simmer for 20 minutes. Add the cannellini beans and simmer for another 20 minutes. Add the barley, beans and peas and simmer for 5–10 minutes until the vegetables are tender. Season with the salt and pepper and grate parmesan cheese over the top to serve.

chickpea, bulgur and parsley salad with marinated lamb

SERVES 4

¼ cup olive oil

2 teaspoons garam masala

14 oz lamb backstrap

sea salt

freshly ground black pepper

7 oz coarse bulgur

14 oz can chickpeas, rinsed

2 fresh green chilies, finely chopped

8 scallions, thinly sliced

large handful fresh Italian parsley, roughly chopped

1 garlic clove, crushed

¼ cup lemon juice

2½ tablespoons pomegranate molasses

Mix 4 teaspoons of the olive oil with the garam masala. Brush all over the lamb, season with the salt and pepper and set aside for 30 minutes.

Put the bulgur in a bowl, cover with hot water and leave to stand for 15 minutes. Drain the bulgur, pressing out as much water as possible.

Put the bulgur, chickpeas, chilli, spring onions and parsley in a bowl and stir together. Cover with plastic wrap and refrigerate. Stir together the garlic, lemon juice, pomegranate molasses, remaining olive oil, salt and pepper to make a dressing.

Preheat the oven to 350°F. Heat a large frying pan over medium-high heat and cook the lamb for 2 minutes on each side, or until browned. Transfer to a roasting pan and roast lamb for 6–7 minutes (for medium). Leave for 10 minutes before carving into thin slices. Drizzle dressing over the salad and serve with the lamb.

Pomegranate molasses is available from Middle Eastern food stores and specialty food stores.

126

spicy chicken thighs with cucumber and cashew salad

¼ cup fish sauce

freshly ground black pepper

3 garlic cloves, crushed

2 large fresh red chilies, finely minced

2 teaspoons sugar

8 boneless, skinless chicken thighs

2½ tablespoons vegetable oil

cucumber and cashew salad

¼ cup lime juice

¼ cup superfine sugar

7 oz vermicelli noodles

2 cucumbers, halved and thinly sliced

small handful of fresh mint

4 scallions, thinly sliced

2½ tablespoons cashew nuts, crushed

Whisk the fish sauce, pepper, garlic, chili and sugar in a bowl. Put the chicken in a separate bowl and pour over half the marinade. Cover with plastic wrap and refrigerate for 20 minutes (keep the rest of the marinade on one side).

Heat the oil in a large frying pan over medium-high heat. Add the chicken, in two batches, and cook for 3 minutes on each side, or until it is cooked through. (Sometimes I put another frying pan on top of the chicken and weigh it down with a couple of cans to make the chicken really crisp.)

While the chicken is cooking, add the lime juice and sugar to the marinade that you set aside. Stir until the sugar has dissolved to make a dressing.

Pour boiling water over the vermicelli and leave for a minute or so until soft. Drain under cold water, place in a large bowl and add the cucumber, mint, spring onions and cashews. Add the dressing, toss well and serve with the sliced chicken.

afternoon tea

As much as fashions change in food, baking is a true constant. Everyone who knows me knows how I love teatime with scones and teacakes, fancy sandwiches and a great smell wafting from the oven. In this hectic world I think it's something we should all enjoy as often as we can.

Even with simple food, afternoon teas feel luxurious. They're a celebration of the homemade in an era of mass production and they're special because they indicate that you're giving time to people you care about. Many of the things I serve for afternoon tea are classics, and they are classics simply because they're good. There's something very honest about baking at home.

I want my family to grow up with good memories around food. A freshly brewed cup of tea with a slice of cake still warm from the oven or a tart made from freshly picked apricots will become part of a happy memory. In fact, nothing makes me happier than filling the house with the warm aroma of freshly baked cakes.

choc banana bread

2 cups all-purpose flour
2 teaspoons baking powder
4½ oz unsalted butter, softened
1 cup superfine sugar
4 ripe bananas, mashed
2 eggs, lightly beaten
1 teaspoon natural vanilla extract
1 cup good-quality dark or milk chocolate chips

to serve
butter

Preheat the oven to 350°F. Sift the flour and baking powder into a large bowl.

Mix the butter, sugar, banana, eggs, vanilla and chocolate chips in a separate bowl. Add to the dry ingredients and stir to combine, being careful not to overmix.

Pour the batter into a non-stick, or lightly greased and floured, 8 x 4 inch loaf pan and bake for 1 hour 15 minutes, or until the bread is cooked when tested with a skewer. Leave to cool in the pan for 5 minutes before turning out onto a wire rack to cool. Serve in thick slices with butter.

When mixing batters, you will often see the words "do not overmix." This is so you don't work the gluten in the flour and toughen the mixture as this makes the end result tough and dry. A loose mixture ensures a moist and delicious result.

plum and vanilla cake

SERVES 10 TO 12

topping
⅓ cup all-purpose flour
3½ oz unsalted butter, chopped
into small pieces
⅓ cup superfine sugar

cake
6¼ oz unsalted butter, softened
1 cup superfine sugar
3 eggs, lightly beaten
1 teaspoon natural vanilla extract
1½ cups all-purpose flour
2 teaspoons baking powder
1 lb 2 oz fresh plums, halved and pitted,
or 1 lb 13 oz canned
plums, pitted

to serve
whipped cream

Preheat the oven to 350°F. To make the topping, place the flour, butter and sugar in a bowl and rub with your fingertips until crumbly (this can be done in a food processor if you prefer).

To make the cake, cream the butter and sugar together in a bowl until light and fluffy. Add the eggs, one at a time, beating well after each addition. Mix in the vanilla. Sift the flour and baking powder into the bowl and fold into the mixture. Spread into a 9 inch greased or non-stick springform cake pan. Top with halved plums with the cut side up. Sprinkle with the topping and bake for 1 hour, or until a skewer inserted into the center of the cake comes out clean.

Remove from the oven and allow to cool in the pan for 10 minutes. Delicious served with whipped cream.

simple scones

4 teaspoons confectioners sugar

2½ cups all-purpose flour

2 tablespoons baking powder

a pinch of salt

1 cup milk

1 oz butter, melted

to serve

jam

lightly whipped cream

Preheat the oven to 425°F. Sift the confectioners sugar, flour, baking powder and salt into a bowl. Add the milk and butter and stir to combine with a knife. Knead quickly and lightly until smooth and then press out to 1¼ inch deep on a floured surface.

Use a glass to cut out rounds roughly 2 inch in diameter and 1¼ inch deep and place them close together on a greased baking pan. Gather the scraps together, lightly knead again, then cut out more rounds. Cook for 8–10 minutes, until puffed and golden. Serve with jam and lightly whipped cream.

When whipping cream, take care to not overwhip. The cream should be still quite soft and wet, not firm and dry.

coconut
blackberry bars

base

4½ oz unsalted butter
¼ cup superfine sugar
1 egg
1 teaspoon natural vanilla extract
1½ cups all-purpose flour
1 teaspoon baking powder
¼ cup milk

filling

½ cup blackberry jam
9 oz blackberries

topping

3½ oz unsalted butter
90 g (7 tablespoons) superfine sugar
2 eggs
2½ cups desiccated coconut
½ cup all-purpose flour

Preheat the oven to 350°F. To make the base, cream the butter and sugar in a bowl until light and fluffy. Add the egg and vanilla and stir with a wooden spoon to combine. Sift the flour and baking powder over the butter mixture, add the milk, and stir to combine.

Flour your hands and press the base evenly into a 12 x 8 inch baking pan, greased and lined with baking paper. Spread the base evenly with jam and sprinkle with blackberries.

To make the topping, cream the butter and sugar in a bowl until light and fluffy. Add the eggs, one at a time, and beat until combined. Stir in the coconut and 1 tablespoon sifted flour, then stir in the remaining flour. Spread the topping evenly over the blackberries.

Bake the slice for 25 minutes, or until golden. Cover with foil and cook for another 10 minutes. Remove from the oven and allow to cool in the pan for 10 minutes. Remove from the pan, cut into rectangles and serve warm or at room temperature.

MAKES 6 strawberry shortcakes

3½ oz cold unsalted butter, cut into
small pieces
2 cups all-purpose flour
¼ cup superfine sugar
4 teaspoons baking powder
a pinch of salt
½ cup cream
1 egg
1 egg yolk, extra
4 teaspoons cream, extra
3 cups strawberries
¼ cup honey
4 teaspoons lemon juice

to serve
heavy cream
confectioners sugar, for sprinkling

Preheat the oven to 400°F. Process the pieces of butter with the flour, sugar, baking powder and salt in a food processor until the mixture resembles coarse breadcrumbs. Transfer to a large bowl.

Mix the cream and egg in a small bowl until combined, then add to the flour and butter mixture and fold in with a knife until just combined. Turn out the dough onto a lightly floured surface and pat out to 1 inch thick. Cut out six rounds with a 2 ¾ inch cutter. Place on a baking sheet lined with parchment paper.

Mix the extra egg yolk and cream and brush on top of the dough rounds. Bake for 20–25 minutes, or until lightly golden. Cool on wire racks for 15 minutes.

While the shortcakes are cooking, hull and slice the strawberries and put them in a bowl. Add the honey and lemon juice and stir to combine.

To serve, slice open each shortcake with a knife and place the bottom halves on a plate. Top each with heavy cream and strawberries, then replace the tops of the shortcakes. Sprinkle with confectioners sugar.

apricot slice

1½ cups all-purpose flour
¾ cup superfine sugar
1 teaspoon baking powder
a pinch of salt
3 eggs
¼ cup milk
2 teaspoons natural vanilla extract
6¼ oz butter, softened
14 apricots, halved and pitted (this may vary depending on the size of the apricots)
2½ tablespoons superfine sugar, extra

Preheat the oven to 315°F. Sift the flour, sugar, baking powder and salt into a large bowl and make a well in the center. Place the eggs, milk and vanilla in another bowl and mix to combine. Pour the egg mixture and butter into the well in the dry ingredients and beat for 2 minutes until smooth. Spread the mixture evenly into a greased or non-stick 8 x 12 inch pan.

Push the apricot halves, cut side up, evenly into the cake mixture in four rows of seven. Place in the oven and bake for 20 minutes, sprinkle over the extra sugar and cook for another 20 minutes, or until a skewer inserted into the center comes out clean. To serve, cut into fingers with two apricot halves per slice.

If fresh apricots are out of season, you can use bottled or canned ones.

145

coconut and lime macadamia cake

1¼ cups macadamia nuts
⅓ cup self-rising flour
a pinch of salt
6 eggs, separated
¾ cup sugar
finely grated zest of 1 lime
½ cup desiccated coconut
lime icing (see below)

Preheat the oven to 350°F. Place the nuts, flour and salt in the bowl of a food processor and process until the nuts are ground. Place the egg yolks and sugar in a bowl and beat for 3 minutes, or until the mixture is pale and creamy. Fold through the zest and coconut then the nut mixture. Place the egg whites in a clean, dry stainless steel bowl and whisk until stiff peaks form. Using a large metal spoon, fold lightly through the nut batter.

Spread the batter evenly into a 9 inch greased or non-stick springform cake pan. Bake for 40 minutes, or until the cake is lightly golden.

Remove from the oven and leave to sit for 10 minutes in the pan. Turn the cake out onto a serving plate. Spread the lime icing over the warm cake, allowing it to drizzle down the sides.

LIME ICING

1 cup confectioners sugar, sifted
2½ tablespoons lime juice
1 teaspoon finely grated lime zest

Combine all the ingredients in a bowl and mix until smooth and glossy.

vanilla cupcakes

4½ oz unsalted butter, softened

1 cup superfine sugar

1½ teaspoons natural vanilla extract

3 eggs

1½ cups all-purpose flour

1 teaspoon baking powder

½ teaspoon salt

¾ cup milk

icing (see below)

fresh raspberries, to decorate

Preheat the oven to 350°F. Line a 12-hole ½ cup capacity muffin pan with paper cups. Place the butter and sugar in a bowl and beat until light and fluffy. Add the vanilla, then add the eggs, one at a time, beating well after each addition. Sift the flour, baking powder and salt and gradually fold into the mixture, alternating with the milk, until it has a soft dropping consistency. Spoon into the cases and bake for 20–25 minutes until golden. Remove from the oven and cool for 10 minutes in the pan. Turn the cakes out onto a wire rack to cool. Ice the cakes when cold and top with raspberries.

ICING

½ cup confectioners sugar, sifted

2–3 teaspoons hot water

a few drops of natural vanilla extract

Place all the ingredients in a bowl and mix until smooth.

mandarin chocolate cake

SERVES 10 TO 12

9 oz good-quality dark chocolate, chopped into small pieces

9 oz unsalted butter, chopped into small pieces

6 eggs, separated

½ cup superfine sugar

¼ cup all-purpose flour, sifted

¼ cup ground almonds

4 teaspoons mandarin zest (if mandarins are out of season, use oranges or tangerines)

to serve

cocoa powder, for dusting

mandarin slices

lightly whipped cream

Preheat the oven to 375°F. Place the chocolate and butter in a heatproof bowl over a saucepan of simmering water, making sure the bowl does not touch the water. Stir the chocolate and butter over the heat until just melted, being careful not to overheat. Remove from the heat and set aside.

Place the egg yolks and sugar in a bowl and mix until lightly combined. Gradually add the melted chocolate to the egg mixture, stirring constantly. Using a large metal spoon, fold through the flour, ground almonds and mandarin zest.

Place the egg whites in a clean, dry stainless steel bowl and whisk until stiff peaks form. Using a large metal spoon, fold half of the egg whites lightly through the batter until barely combined. Fold through the remaining egg whites, again barely combining.

Pour the batter into a 9 inch greased or non-stick springform cake pan and bake for 35 minutes. Don't worry if the cake still seems to be very wet in the center: it will firm up a little on cooling.

Remove the cake from the oven and leave to cool completely in the pan. Transfer to a serving platter and dust with the cocoa powder. Serve with the mandarin slices and lightly whipped cream.

banana maple upside-down cake

1¾ oz unsalted butter

¼ cup soft brown sugar

¼ cup maple syrup

3–4 bananas, peeled and sliced in half lengthways

3½ oz unsalted butter, softened, extra

1 cup superfine sugar

4 eggs

1 teaspoon natural vanilla extract

1¼ cup all-purpose flour

1 teaspoon baking powder

a pinch of salt

to serve

vanilla ice cream (optional)

Preheat the oven to 350°F. To make the topping, place the butter, brown sugar and maple syrup in a small saucepan. Cook over a medium heat for 10 minutes, or until the sugar melts and the syrup is rich and golden. Pour the syrup into a 9 inch greased or non-stick springform cake pan and arrange the sliced bananas, cut side down, over the base of the pan.

To make the cake, place the extra butter and superfine sugar in a bowl and beat until pale and creamy. Add the eggs one at a time, beating after each addition, then add the vanilla.

Sift the flour, baking powder and salt and gently fold through the mixture. Spoon the batter evenly over the bananas and caramel and smooth the top with a spatula.

Place the cake in the oven on a baking sheet to catch any escaping caramel and bake for 35 minutes, or until a skewer inserted into the center of the cake comes out clean.

Remove from the oven and leave in the pan for 5 minutes to cool slightly. Transfer to a large serving plate. Serve warm with vanilla ice cream, if desired.

This recipe can also be made very successfully with granny smith apples. Cook the sliced apples in the caramel for 5 minutes before placing in the pan and topping with the cake mixture.

friands

1⅓ cups ground almonds
1¾ cups confectioners sugar, sifted
⅔ cup all-purpose flour, sifted
8 egg whites
5½ oz unsalted butter, melted
1½ cups cherries or 1 cup raspberries or 3 nectarines, chopped
confectioners sugar, extra, for dusting

Preheat the oven to 350°F. Grease and flour a non-stick 12-hole friand pan. Mix together the ground almonds, icing sugar and flour. Stir in the egg whites until just combined. Stir in the melted butter.

Pour the batter into the pan. Pit the cherries and cut in half. Arrange a few cherry halves or raspberries or nectarine pieces on top of each friand.

Bake for 25–30 minutes or until pale and golden. The friands should spring back when touched. Remove from the oven and leave in the pan for 5 minutes before turning out onto a wire rack to cool. Dust with extra confectioners sugar and store in an airtight container.

buttermilk cake with raspberry syrup

SERVES 8 TO 10

4½ oz unsalted butter, softened

1 cup superfine sugar

2 eggs

1 cup buttermilk

1 teaspoon natural vanilla extract

2 cups all-purpose flour

2 teaspoons baking powder

a pinch of salt

raspberry syrup (see below)

to serve

lightly whipped cream

raspberries

Preheat the oven to 350°F. Using electric beaters, cream the butter and sugar until pale and fluffy. Add the eggs, one at a time, beating well after each addition. With the mixer at low speed, beat in the buttermilk and the vanilla until just combined. Sift in the flour, baking powder and salt in two batches, mixing well after each addition.

Spoon the mixture into a 8 inch cake pan, greased and lined with parchment paper, and smooth the top. Bake for 45–50 minutes, or until a skewer comes out clean. Leave to cool in the pan for 10 minutes, then transfer to a plate and pour syrup over the top.

Place slices of cake on serving plates with some lightly whipped cream and raspberries.

RASPBERRY SYRUP

½ cup sugar

2½ tablespoons lemon juice

7¾ oz raspberries

Stir the sugar, lemon juice and ¼ cup water in a saucepan over a medium to high heat until the sugar dissolves. Cook for 2–3 minutes, then add the raspberries and lightly crush with the back of a spoon. Cook for another 3 minutes, then remove from the heat and purée in a blender.

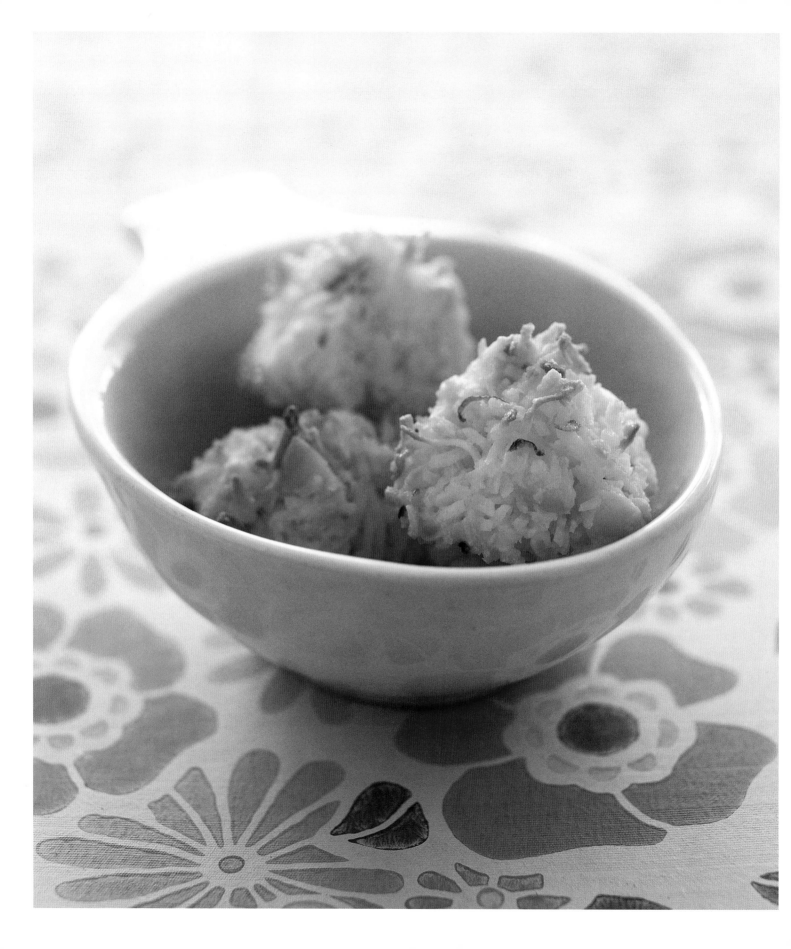

coconut macaroons

2 egg whites
½ cup superfine sugar
2 cups shredded coconut
¾ cup roughly chopped macadamia nuts
1 teaspoon lime zest

Preheat the oven to 315°F. Mix together egg whites, sugar, coconut, nuts and lime zest in a bowl (you may need to use your hands).

Shape tablespoons of the mixture into mounds on baking sheets lined with parchment paper. Bake for 10–15 minutes or until light golden brown. Cool on the trays.

I sometimes serve coconut macaroons as a dessert with a scoop of coconut ice cream.

MAKES 24 apricot bars

1¼ cups all-purpose flour
½ cup soft brown sugar
½ cup superfine sugar
2 pinches of salt
1 teaspoon baking powder
6 oz unsalted butter, chilled and diced
1 cup old-fashioned oats
1 cup desiccated coconut
2½ cups dried apricots, chopped
⅓ cup apricot jam
1½ oz unsalted butter, extra, melted

Preheat the oven to 350°F. Mix the flour, sugars, salt, baking powder and butter in a food processor until a dough forms. (Or, rub the ingredients together with your fingertips.) Mix in the oats and coconut. Reserve a cupful of dough and press the remainder evenly into a 8 x 12 inch baking pan, lightly greased and lined with parchment paper. Bake for 15 minutes, or until golden.

Put the apricots and ½ cup of water in a small saucepan over low heat and cook, stirring occasionally, until the liquid has been absorbed. Cool slightly, then spoon over the dough base. Dot the jam over the apricots and crumble the reserved dough over the top. Spoon on the melted butter and bake for 30–35 minutes until lightly golden. Leave to cool completely on the sheet. Slice into squares and store in an airtight container.

peach and raspberry bars

1½ cups all-purpose flour

1½ teaspoons baking powder, plus
½ teaspoon extra

4½ oz butter, chilled and diced

½ cup soft brown sugar

½ cup superfine sugar

3 ripe peaches, peeled and sliced into wedges
(see below)

¾ cup raspberries, fresh
or frozen

2 teaspoons natural vanilla extract

1 egg, lightly beaten

¾ cup milk

Preheat the oven to 350°F. Grease and line the base of a 8 × 12 inch baking pan with parchment paper. Sift flour and baking powder into a large bowl and then rub in the butter with your fingertips. Stir in both the sugars. Press half the mixture over the base of the pan. Lay peaches over top and sprinkle with raspberries.

Add the vanilla, extra baking powder, egg and milk to the rest of the base mixture and stir well – don't worry too much about lumps. Pour evenly over the top of the peaches and raspberries and bake for 1 hour. Cool in the tray, then cut into squares to serve.

To peel peaches, score a cross in the skin with a sharp knife, then blanch the peaches in boiling water for 30 seconds, refresh in cold water and peel the skin away from the cross.

MAKES 16 lamingtons

sponge cake
6 eggs
⅔ cup superfine sugar
1⅔ cups self-rising flour
1 oz unsalted butter, melted

chocolate icing
4 cups confectioners sugar
1⅓ cups dark chocolate, chopped
½ oz unsalted butter
½ cup milk
4 cups desiccated coconut

Preheat the oven to 350°F. Lightly grease and line the base of an 7 x 11 inch baking pan with parchment paper.

To make the cake, whisk the eggs for about 5 minutes with an electric mixer until light and fluffy. Gradually add the sugar and continue beating until the mixture is thick and the sugar has dissolved. Sift over the flour and fold in lightly. Add the butter and ¼ cup of hot water and stir gently to combine. Pour into the pan and bake for 30 minutes, or until golden. Cool on a wire rack.

To make the chocolate icing, put the sugar, dark chocolate, butter and milk in a heatproof bowl and place over a saucepan of simmering water. Stir constantly until melted and combined.

Cut the cake into 16 squares. Put the coconut in a bowl. Dip each cake square into the chocolate icing and then in the coconut. Leave on a wire rack to dry completely before serving.

fresh apricot and cinnamon cake

5 oz self-rising flour

½ teaspoon ground cinnamon

¼ cup superfine sugar

1 egg, lightly beaten

¼ cup milk

1 teaspoon natural vanilla extract

3 oz unsalted butter, melted

12 oz fresh apricots, halved and pitted

topping

⅓ cup all-purpose flour

1 teaspoon ground cinnamon

1¼ oz superfine sugar

1¼ oz unsalted butter, chilled and diced

Preheat the oven to 350°F. Grease and line the base of an 8 inch round spring-form cake pan with parchment paper. Sift the flour and cinnamon into a large bowl and stir in the sugar. Make a well in the center and pour in the egg, milk, vanilla and melted butter. Mix with a wooden spoon until the batter is smooth, then spoon into the pan. Arrange the apricots, cut side up, evenly over the batter and then gently press them down.

For the topping, put the flour, cinnamon and sugar in a bowl. Rub in the butter with your fingertips until crumbs form. Scatter the topping evenly over the apricots.

Bake for 35–40 minutes, or until the cake is light golden and a skewer inserted into the center comes out clean. Leave to cool in the pan for 10 minutes before transferring to a wire rack to cool completely.

almond and raspberry bar

topping
2½ oz unsalted butter, softened
¼ cup superfine sugar
1 teaspoon natural vanilla extract
7 oz flaked almonds
2½ tablespoons milk

base
5½ oz unsalted butter, softened
½ cup superfine sugar
1 teaspoon natural vanilla extract
1¾ cups all-purpose flour
⅓ cup cornstarch

filling
½ cup raspberry jam

Preheat the oven to 350°F. Lightly grease a 9 x 9 inch baking pan and line with parchment paper.

To make the almond topping, put the butter, sugar, vanilla, almonds and milk in a saucepan. Cook over a very low heat until the butter has melted, then leave to cool.

To make the base, beat the butter, sugar and vanilla with electric beaters until pale and creamy. Sift the flour and cornstarch together and add in two batches, beating on low speed until just mixed. Press the dough into the baking pan and bake for 12 minutes, or until light golden. Remove from the oven and leave to cool for 10 minutes.

Carefully spread the jam over the pastry base, then spread the cooled almond topping over the jam. Return to the oven and bake for a further 25 minutes, or until golden brown.

170

chocolate caramel squares

1 cup all-purpose flour
1 teaspoon baking powder
1 cup desiccated coconut
½ cup superfine sugar
4½ oz unsalted butter, melted

filling
3½ oz unsalted butter
3½ oz brown sugar
14 fl oz can condensed milk
2½ tablespoons golden syrup
1 teaspoon natural vanilla extract

topping
5½ oz good-quality dark chocolate
1 teaspoon flaked sea salt, such as Maldon sea salt

Preheat the oven to 350°F and lightly grease and line a 7 × 11 inch baking pan with parchment paper.

Sift the flour and baking powder into a large bowl, add the coconut, sugar and melted butter and stir together well. Press firmly into the base of the pan and bake for 12 minutes, or until light golden.

To make the filling, put the butter, brown sugar, condensed milk, golden syrup and vanilla in a saucepan over a low heat. Cook, stirring, until the sugar has dissolved. Bring to a boil, then reduce the heat to low and cook, stirring, for 5 minutes, or until light golden. Pour evenly over the cooked base, then return to the oven and bake for 10 minutes. Set aside to cool completely.

Once the caramel is cool, put the chocolate in a heatproof bowl over a saucepan of gently simmering water, stirring occasionally until the chocolate has melted (or melt the chocolate very carefully in a microwave oven). Spread the chocolate evenly over the caramel. Once the chocolate has set, sprinkle with the sea salt and cut into squares.

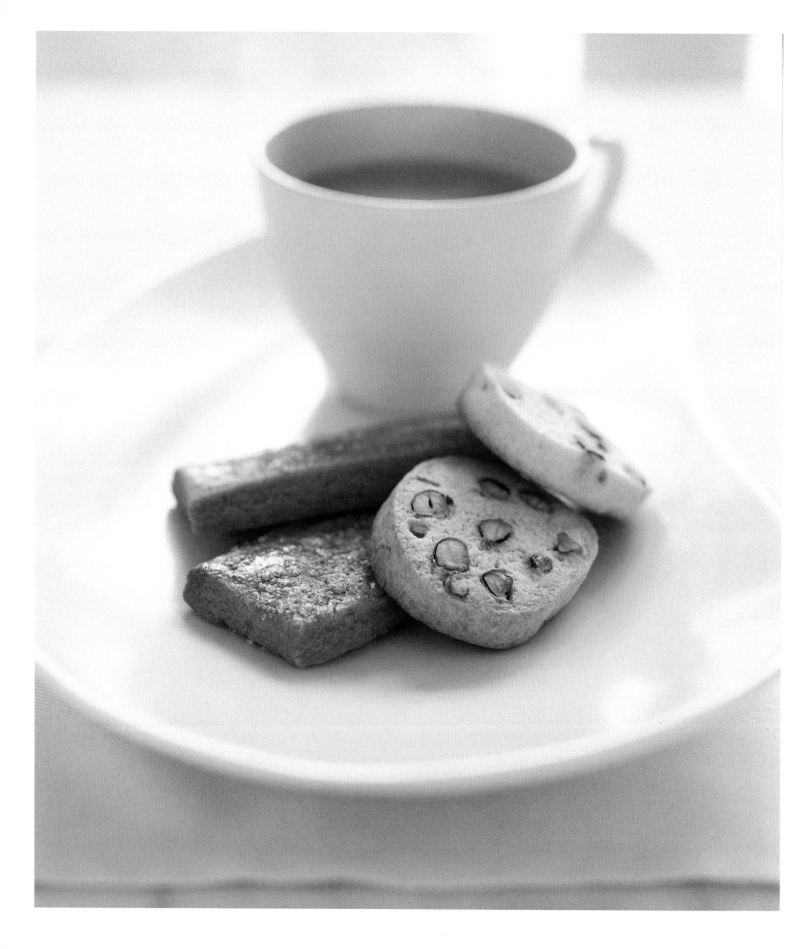

bill's cookies

PISTACHIO COOKIES

4½ oz shelled pistachios
4½ oz unsalted butter, softened
½ cup superfine sugar
1 egg
4 teaspoons rosewater
1½ cups all-purpose flour, sifted
1 teaspoon baking powder, sifted
2½ tablespoons all-purpose flour, extra

Place the pistachios in a small bowl, cover with water and set aside for 30 minutes. (It is important to soak the pistachios so you can slice through them when cutting the dough.) Place the butter and sugar in a bowl and beat until pale and creamy. Add the egg and mix until combined. Add the rosewater, and stir until smooth. Drain the pistachios well then add to the batter with the flour and baking powder. Fold through until a stiff dough forms.

Sift the extra flour over a clean dry surface, and knead the dough lightly for 30 seconds. Divide the dough in half and roll each into a log, roughly 2 inches in diameter. Wrap each log in plastic wrap and refrigerate for 30 minutes.

Preheat the oven to 350°F. Remove the dough from the refrigerator, and slice into ¼ inch rounds. Place cookies ¾ inch apart on a baking sheet lined with parchment paper. Bake for 10–12 minutes, or until lightly golden. Remove from the oven and leave to cool on a wire rack.

ORANGE AND CARDAMOM COOKIES

3 cups all-purpose flour
2 teaspoons baking powder
4 teaspoons ground ginger
1 teaspoon ground nutmeg
1 teaspoon ground cardamom
9 oz unsalted butter, softened
1½ cups soft brown sugar
1 tablespoon brandy
finely grated zest of 1 orange
¼ cup all-purpose flour, extra
1 egg white, for glazing
1 oz granulated sugar

Sift the flour, baking powder, ginger, nutmeg and cardamom into a large bowl. Place the butter and brown sugar in a bowl and beat until pale and creamy. Add the brandy and zest and mix well. Using a large metal spoon, fold the dry ingredients through in two batches.

Sift the extra flour over a clean dry surface and knead the dough for 30 seconds. Roll the dough into a large rectangle ¼ inch thick. Cut into shapes 1¼ x 2½ inches long. Brush with the egg white and sprinkle with sugar.

Preheat the oven to 350°F. Place the cookies ¾ inch apart on a baking sheet lined with parchment paper. Bake for 10–12 minutes, or until lightly browned. Remove from the oven and leave to cool on a wire rack.

175

dinner

The older I get the more simply I like to eat and the more I appreciate uncomplicated things. But, if I have time, I enjoy making a complicated dinner with the day spent shopping and cooking something challenging. I also love an appreciative audience when cooking. Having said that, I'm not hugely in favor of formal dinners and I rarely serve a three-course, sit-down meal.

I love it when I'm invited to someone else's house for dinner, but I don't get asked that often. I suspect people are afraid of what I might think of their cooking. If only they knew it's not the food that makes or breaks an occasion. Being a good host is about enjoying yourself as well as entertaining others.

I often get asked what makes a great dinner party and I think the best advice I can give is very simple. Be realistic about your time (everything will always take longer than you think) and invite the right mix of people. I've met most of my closest friends over a dinner table.

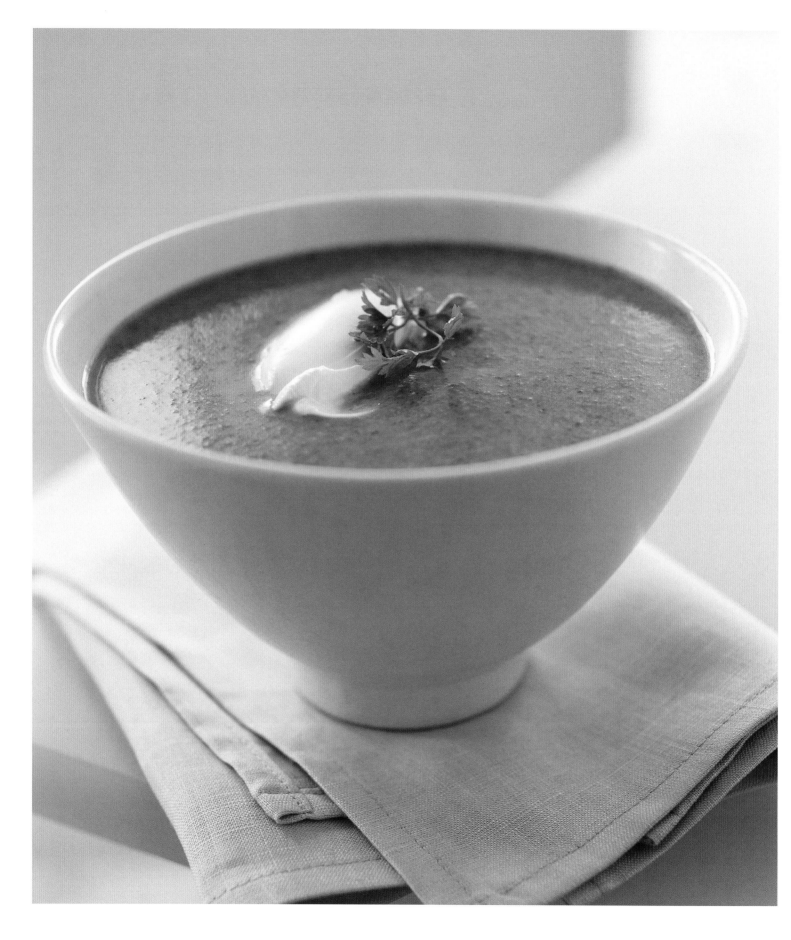

mushroom soup

12 oz button mushrooms
9 oz potatoes, peeled and
roughly chopped
1 oz butter
2½ tablespoons olive oil
2 garlic cloves, finely chopped
sea salt
freshly ground black pepper
½ cup dry white wine
2 teaspoons finely chopped fresh oregano
6 cups chicken stock or water

to serve
fresh parsley sprigs
⅓ cup sour cream (optional)

Finely chop the mushrooms in a food processor using the pulse action. Remove and repeat the process with the potatoes.

Heat the butter and oil in a large saucepan over a medium heat. Add the mushrooms, garlic and a little salt and pepper, and cook for 10 minutes. Add the potato, wine, oregano and stock and bring to a boil over a high heat. Reduce the heat to low and simmer for 25 minutes. Let the soup cool slightly, then transfer 1½ cups of the soup to a blender and blend until smooth. Return to the saucepan and stir well.

Ladle into serving bowls, top with a sprig of parsley and a tablespoon of sour cream, if you wish.

To change the flavor of this soup, just use different types of mushrooms. Darker ones will give a richer flavor, whereas lighter ones will give a more delicate flavor.

SERVES 4 garlic shrimp

20 raw king shrimp, peeled, deveined and
tails left intact

1 cup olive oil

5 garlic cloves, finely chopped

3 small fresh red chilies, split lengthways
but intact at stem

1 teaspoon sea salt

freshly ground black pepper

2½ tablespoons chopped fresh
Italian parsley

to serve
lemon wedges
crusty bread
green salad

Preheat the oven to 500°F. Cut a slit down the back of each shrimp and place the shrimp in an ovenproof dish that will hold them snugly in a single layer.

Heat the oil in a large ovenproof frying pan over a high heat. Add half the garlic and all the chilies and cook for 1 minute or until the garlic starts to change color. Pour over the shrimp, then sprinkle with the remaining garlic. Season with the salt and pepper, cover with foil and bake for 10 minutes, or until the shrimp are pink and cooked through. Don't overcook — remember that the shrimp will continue cooking after being removed from the oven. Serve in a large bowl or divide among four serving dishes. Sprinkle with parsley and serve with lemon wedges, crusty bread and a green salad.

spaghetti with spicy meatballs

$\frac{1}{3}$ cup milk

1 slice of bread, crust removed

1 lb 2 oz ground beef, or pork and veal

1 small onion, finely chopped

2$\frac{1}{2}$ tablespoons fresh Italian parsley, chopped

1 teaspoon fresh thyme, finely chopped

1 egg, lightly beaten

$\frac{1}{4}$ cup freshly grated parmesan cheese

2 garlic cloves, finely crushed

2 fresh red chilies, finely chopped

sea salt

freshly ground black pepper

$\frac{1}{4}$ cup olive oil

2 x 14 oz cans chopped tomatoes

$\frac{1}{2}$ cup fresh basil leaves, shredded

1 lb 2 oz spaghetti

to serve

a handful of fresh basil leaves, extra

freshly grated parmesan cheese

Put the milk and bread in a small saucepan and place over a low heat. When the bread has absorbed the milk, remove from the heat and mash with a fork. Allow to cool.

Combine the meat, onion, parsley, thyme, egg, parmesan, garlic, half of the chili, the bread mixture and lots of salt and pepper in a large bowl. Gently mix with your hands, then shape into small balls. I find wetting my hands makes this easier.

Heat the oil in a large frying pan over a medium heat and, when hot, add the meatballs. Brown the meatballs on all sides, turning carefully. Alternatively, you can toss the meatballs in oil in a roasting pan and bake them at 425°F for 10–15 minutes. You may find this easier because the meatballs won't break up. Drain off any excess oil (if you've baked the meatballs, transfer them to a frying pan) and add the tomatoes, remaining chili, basil and salt and pepper. Stir the meatballs carefully to coat with the tomatoes, then simmer for 20 minutes.

While the meatballs are cooking, cook the pasta in a large pot of rapidly boiling salted water until *al dente*. Drain well.

To serve, divide the drained spaghetti among four bowls and spoon over the meatballs and sauce. Sprinkle with extra basil leaves and serve with freshly grated parmesan cheese.

rare roast beef fillet with roasted tomatoes and mustard cream

SERVES 4

3 lb 5 oz center-cut beef fillet
sea salt
freshly ground black pepper
2½ tablespoons olive oil
1 bunch watercress

to serve
roasted tomatoes (see below)
mustard cream (see below)
mashed potatoes

Preheat the oven to 475°F. Season the beef fillet with salt and pepper. Heat a large frying pan over a high heat and add the oil. When very hot, sear the beef on all sides until browned, then transfer to a roasting pan. Roast the beef, allowing 7 minutes per 1 lb 2 oz for rare, and 10 minutes per 1 lb 2 oz for medium. Remove from the oven and allow to rest in a warm place, covered with foil, for 7 minutes.

Pick the leaves off the watercress and discard the stalks. Cut the meat into thick slices and serve with the watercress, roasted tomatoes and some mashed potatoes. Drizzle with pan juices and serve with mustard cream.

ROASTED TOMATOES

4 ripe tomatoes, halved lengthways
sea salt
freshly ground black pepper
2 garlic cloves, finely sliced
¼ cup fresh breadcrumbs
2½ tablespoons fresh Italian parsley, finely chopped
2½ tablespoons extra virgin olive oil

Preheat the oven to 400°F. Arrange the tomatoes with the cut sides up in a small roasting pan. Season with salt and pepper and sprinkle with garlic slices. Stir the breadcrumbs and parsley together in a bowl. Scatter over the tomatoes and drizzle with olive oil, then cook for 45 minutes.

MUSTARD CREAM

4 teaspoons dijon mustard
½ cup crème fraîche
or sour cream
1 teaspoon lemon juice
sea salt
freshly ground black pepper

Place all the ingredients in a bowl and stir to combine.

186

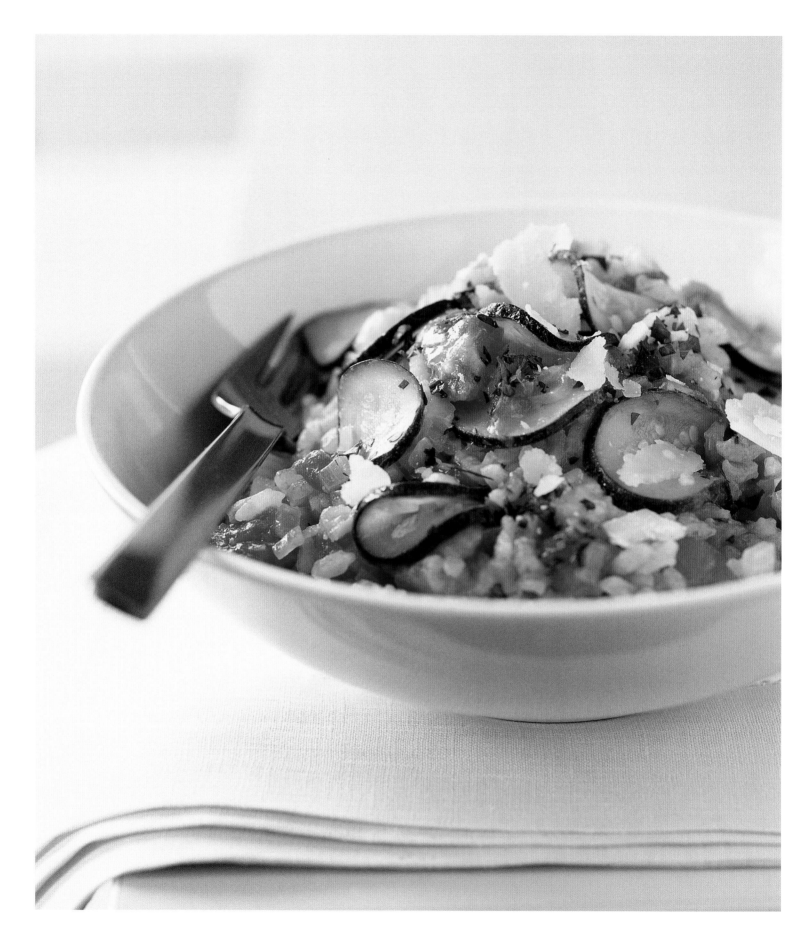

baked risotto with zucchini, tomato and parmesan

SERVES 4

2½ tablespoons extra virgin olive oil

1 onion, finely chopped

1 teaspoon sea salt

1 cup arborio rice

1½ cups chicken stock or water

14 oz can chopped tomatoes

3 zucchini, thinly sliced

2¼ oz freshly grated parmesan cheese

freshly ground black pepper

2½ tablespoons finely chopped fresh Italian parsley

shavings of parmesan cheese, for serving (optional)

Preheat the oven to 400°F. Heat a 12 cup capacity flameproof casserole dish (with a lid) over a medium heat. Add the olive oil, onion and salt and stir for 5 minutes, or until the onion is soft and translucent.

Add the rice to the dish and stir for another minute. Add the stock or water and the chopped tomatoes and bring to simmering point. Stir in the zucchini and sprinkle with parmesan cheese and black pepper. Cover the dish and bake the risotto for 30 minutes, or until the rice is cooked. Scatter parsley over the top, sprinkle with parmesan shavings, if desired.

You can use this risotto as a base for other flavors — try replacing the zucchini with canned tuna, or even a mixture of seafood. When using seafood I like to omit the parmesan cheese.

189

linguine with clams and tomatoes

SERVES 4 TO 6

14 oz good-quality Italian
dried linguine

¼ cup extra virgin olive oil

3 garlic cloves, thinly sliced

2 small fresh red chilies, finely chopped, or
½ teaspoon dried chili flakes

sea salt

2 lb 4 oz clams

½ cup white wine

1 lb 2 oz cherry tomatoes, cut
into halves

¼ cup fresh parsley, finely chopped

freshly ground black pepper

Cook the linguine in a large saucepan of rapidly boiling salted water until *al dente*.

While the pasta is cooking, heat the olive oil in a large deep frying pan over a medium heat.

Add the garlic, chili and salt and cook gently for 1 minute. Add the clams, white wine and tomatoes. Cover the pan and cook for 3 minutes, or until the clams open. Discard any unopened clams. Remove from the heat.

Drain the pasta and add to the frying pan with the parsley. Gently toss to combine, then season with salt and pepper, to taste.

To get clams to spit out any grit they might have hidden in their shells, put them in a bowl of cold water with some oats or polenta. Rinse well before use.

baked polenta with a simple tomato sauce

4 teaspoons sea salt
1½ cups instant polenta
4 teaspoons extra virgin olive oil
simple tomato sauce (see below)
12 oz ricotta cheese
¼ cup finely grated parmesan cheese
freshly ground black pepper

Put 6 cups water in a large saucepan over a high heat and bring to the boil. Add the salt and pour the polenta, constantly stirring with a wooden spoon, into the water in a steady stream. Reduce the heat to low, cover and cook for another 10 minutes, stirring regularly.

Lightly oil a 12 x 8 inch baking dish with half the olive oil. Pour the cooked polenta into the prepared dish and spread evenly. Leave to cool and firm in the baking dish then turn out onto a cutting board. Cut the polenta into 5 cm (2 inch) squares.

Preheat the oven to 400°F. Lightly grease an 8 x 10 inch gratin dish or four individual dishes with the remaining oil. Place the polenta squares in a single layer, slightly overlapping. Pour the simple tomato sauce evenly over the polenta. Crumble the ricotta and sprinkle parmesan cheese over the top. Season with pepper. Bake for 30 minutes, or until golden.

SIMPLE TOMATO SAUCE

2 x 14 oz cans chopped tomatoes
2½ tablespoons extra virgin olive oil
1 teaspoon sea salt
1 teaspoon sugar
freshly ground black pepper
2 garlic cloves, crushed

Place the tomatoes in a saucepan over a medium heat and cook for 15 minutes, stirring occasionally. Add the remaining ingredients, cook for 1 minute then remove from the heat.

Polenta is thick and sticky and needs to be stirred regularly so it doesn't catch on the base of the pan.

stir-fried mussels with chili and black bean

2 teaspoons sugar

2½ tablespoons soy sauce

¼ cup shaoxing rice wine, or dry sherry

2½ tablespoons vegetable oil

¼ cup fresh ginger, thinly sliced

4 scallions, sliced into 2 inch lengths

4 garlic cloves, crushed

2 large fresh red chilies, halved lengthways

2½ tablespoons fermented black beans, rinsed and crushed

2 lb 4 oz mussels, scrubbed and debearded

to serve

steamed rice

Place the sugar, soy sauce, shaoxing rice wine and ¼ cup water in a small bowl and stir to combine. Heat a large wok or wide, flat saucepan until very hot, add the oil and when hot add the ginger, spring onion, garlic, chili and black beans and stir for 30 seconds until aromatic. Add the mussels and toss to combine. Pour over the soy mixture, and cover. Cook covered for 2–5 minutes, shaking the pan, until the mussels open. Shake all the mussels, discarding any unopened ones, and sauce into a large warmed serving dish. Serve with steamed rice.

To prepare mussels, I scrub them under running water with a clean kitchen scourer which works marvelously to remove any residual seaweed or slime. Remove the beard. Discard any with broken shells and ones that don't close when tapped lightly on the bench.

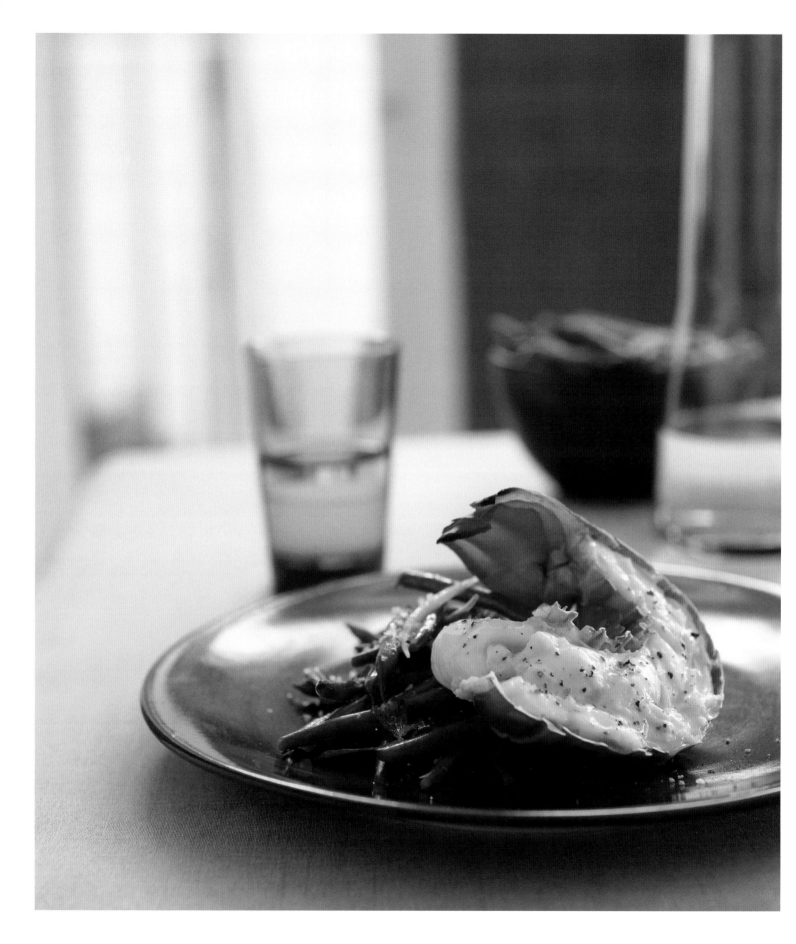

lobster with lime butter

¼ cup lime juice
4½ oz butter, chopped
2 large raw lobster tails in the shell
sea salt
freshly ground black pepper
4 teaspoons olive oil

to serve
green bean salad (see below)

Place a baking tray in the oven and preheat to 425°F. To make the lime butter, heat the lime juice in a small saucepan over a medium heat. Add the butter and whisk constantly until melted. Set aside. Cut the lobster tails in half lengthways and season with salt and pepper. Place a large frying pan over a high heat, add the oil and arrange the lobsters cut side down in the pan. Sear for 2 minutes, place the lobsters on the hot baking sheet, drizzle with lime butter and roast for 10–15 minutes, or until the lobster flesh is opaque and just cooked. Arrange the lobster tails on a platter and serve with green bean salad.

GREEN BEAN SALAD

1 lb 2 oz green beans, topped
1 teaspoon wholegrain mustard
¼ cup extra virgin olive oil
4 teaspoons red wine vinegar
sea salt
freshly ground black pepper
½ red onion, finely sliced
1 cup fresh Italian parsley

Blanch the beans in boiling water for 2 minutes, or until just tender and bright green in color. Drain and refresh under cold water.

Place the mustard, olive oil and vinegar in a large bowl and whisk to combine. Season with salt and pepper. Add the beans, onion and parsley and gently toss to combine.

caramel chicken

SERVES 4

8 chicken thigh fillets, skinless,
chopped in half
4 teaspoons vegetable oil
1 red onion, sliced
3 garlic cloves, sliced
freshly ground black pepper
¼ cup dark soy sauce
½ cup soft brown sugar
¼ cup fish sauce

to serve
steamed rice
steamed green vegetables, such as snow
peas, asparagus or
Chinese broccoli (gai larn)

Place the chicken and oil in a bowl and toss to combine. Heat a large frying pan over a high heat until hot. Cook the chicken, in two batches, for 2 minutes on one side until lightly brown, turn and cook for another minute. Remove from the pan.

Reduce the heat to medium and add a little extra oil if needed. Add the onion and garlic and cook for 5 minutes, stirring occasionally. Return the chicken to the pan, sprinkle liberally with black pepper, add the soy sauce and stir to combine. Cover the pan, reduce heat to low and cook for 10 minutes, stirring occasionally. Increase the heat to high, add the sugar and stir to combine. Cook uncovered for 3–4 minutes, or until the sauce is rich, dark and syrupy and the chicken is cooked. Add the fish sauce and stir to combine. Place in a serving dish and serve with steamed rice and green vegetables.

marinated lamb with spicy eggplant salad

SERVES 4

1 teaspoon paprika

½ teaspoon ground cumin

2 garlic cloves, crushed

2½ tablespoons olive oil

4 x 7 oz lamb backstraps

sea salt

freshly ground black pepper

to serve

spicy eggplant salad (see below)

fresh cilantro sprigs

plain yogurt

2 large eggplants

2½ tablespoons olive oil

3 garlic cloves, crushed

¼ cup fresh Italian parsley, chopped

¼ cup fresh cilantro leaves, chopped

2 tablespoons paprika

1 small fresh red chili, seeded and finely chopped

½ teaspoon ground cumin

2½ tablespoons olive oil, extra

4 large plum tomatoes, roughly chopped

1 teaspoon sea salt

4 teaspoons soft brown sugar

2½ tablespoons lemon juice

4 teaspoons red wine vinegar

freshly ground black pepper

Place the paprika, cumin, garlic and olive oil in a bowl and stir to combine. Trim the lamb of any excess fat and sinew then coat with the marinade. Cover with plastic wrap and place in the refrigerator to marinate for 2 hours, bringing to room temperature in the last 30 minutes.

Heat a frying pan over a high heat. Season the lamb with salt and pepper and cook for 3–4 minutes each side. Transfer the lamb to a plate, cover with foil and keep in a warm place for 10 minutes. Slice each lamb fillet on the diagonal into ¾ inch pieces and serve with the spicy eggplant salad, coriander sprigs and yogurt.

SPICY EGGPLANT SALAD

Cut the eggplant into ½ inch thick slices. Preheat the oven to 400°F. Place the eggplant in a single layer on two baking sheets and brush with olive oil on each side. Cook for 30 minutes, swapping the position of the sheets halfway through. Remove from the oven. Sprinkle the eggplant with water if it is a little dry. Cool for 5 minutes, dice and place in a bowl. Add the garlic, parsley, cilantro, paprika, chili and cumin and stir to combine. Place the extra olive oil in a saucepan over a medium to high heat and add the tomatoes, salt and sugar. Cook for 10 minutes, add the eggplant mixture and cook for another 5 minutes. Remove from the heat and stir in the lemon juice, vinegar and pepper. Serve warm.

stuffed roast chicken

6 thick slices good-quality bread (I like whole wheat)

4 teaspoons olive oil

1 cup onion, roughly chopped

2¾ oz pancetta, bacon or prosciutto, chopped

zest of 1 lemon, finely grated

4 teaspoons fresh sage or thyme, chopped

¼ cup fresh italian parsley, roughly chopped

sea salt

freshly ground black pepper

1 egg, lightly beaten

3 lb 5 oz free-range chicken

4 teaspoons olive oil, extra

to serve

roast vegetables (see below)

green salad (optional)

Preheat the oven to 425°F. Tear the bread roughly and place in a food processor and process until large breadcrumbs form. Place in a large bowl.

Place a frying pan over a medium heat. Put the olive oil in the pan, heat and add the onion. Cook for 3 minutes, stirring occasionally. Add the pancetta and cook for another 3 minutes. Remove the onion and pancetta and place in the bowl of breadcrumbs. Add the zest, sage, parsley, salt, pepper and egg and mix well to combine.

Wash the chicken and dry inside and out with paper towels. Fill the cavity with the stuffing mixture, then truss the chicken with kitchen string. Rub lightly with extra olive oil then season with salt and pepper.

Place the chicken in the oven, breast side up, and cook for 15 minutes. Lower the heat to 350°F and cook for another hour, or until the juices run clear when a skewer is inserted into the thickest part of the thigh. Remove from the oven, loosely cover with foil and rest for 15 minutes before carving. Serve with a green salad, if desired, and the roast vegetables.

ROAST VEGETABLES

2 lb 4 oz winter squash, potato and sweet potato, cut into chunks

2 red onions, peeled and quartered

¼ cup extra virgin olive oil

sea salt

freshly ground black pepper

Place all the ingredients in a bowl and toss to combine. Put into a baking dish, spreading the vegetables evenly, and bake at the same time as the chicken. Leave in the oven while the chicken is resting.

veal cutlets with tomatoes, capers and polenta

SERVES 4

4 large ripe tomatoes, each cut into eight wedges

4 teaspoons fresh oregano

2½ tablespoons capers, rinsed and squeezed dry

2 garlic cloves, sliced

1 red onion, cut into fine wedges

2½ tablespoons olive oil, plus extra for brushing

sea salt

freshly ground black pepper

4 veal cutlets

to serve

polenta (see below)

4 teaspoons salt

1⅔ cups polenta

½ cup freshly grated parmesan cheese

Preheat the oven to 400°F. If you intend to serve these cutlets with polenta, start cooking your polenta now.

Put the tomatoes, oregano, capers, garlic, onion and olive oil in a small roasting tin (large enough to fit the veal cutlets) and toss together. Sprinkle with salt and pepper. Cover with foil and bake for 25–30 minutes. Remove the foil and bake for another 10 minutes.

While the tomatoes are cooking, brush the veal cutlets with oil and season liberally with salt and pepper. Heat a large frying pan over a high heat for 1–2 minutes, until very hot. Add the veal cutlets and cook for 1 minute on each side, or until the veal is sealed. Remove from the pan. Place the veal cutlets on top of the tomatoes and bake for 10–15 minutes, until the veal is cooked. Serve with polenta.

POLENTA

To make the polenta, you'll need a large heatproof bowl that will sit over a large saucepan. Fill the saucepan two-thirds with water but make sure the base of the bowl will not touch the water. Bring the water to a boil. Pour 7 cups extra boiling water into the bowl, add the salt and polenta and whisk continuously for about 4 minutes, until the mixture thickens. Cover the bowl tightly with foil and sit the bowl over the saucepan of steadily boiling water. After 20 minutes, remove the bowl, carefully lift off the foil and thoroughly stir the polenta. Cover again and return to the heat. Do this every 20 minutes. Check the boiling water underneath as well, topping up as necessary. The polenta should be ready after it has cooked for 1½ hours. Stir in the parmesan cheese just before serving.

206

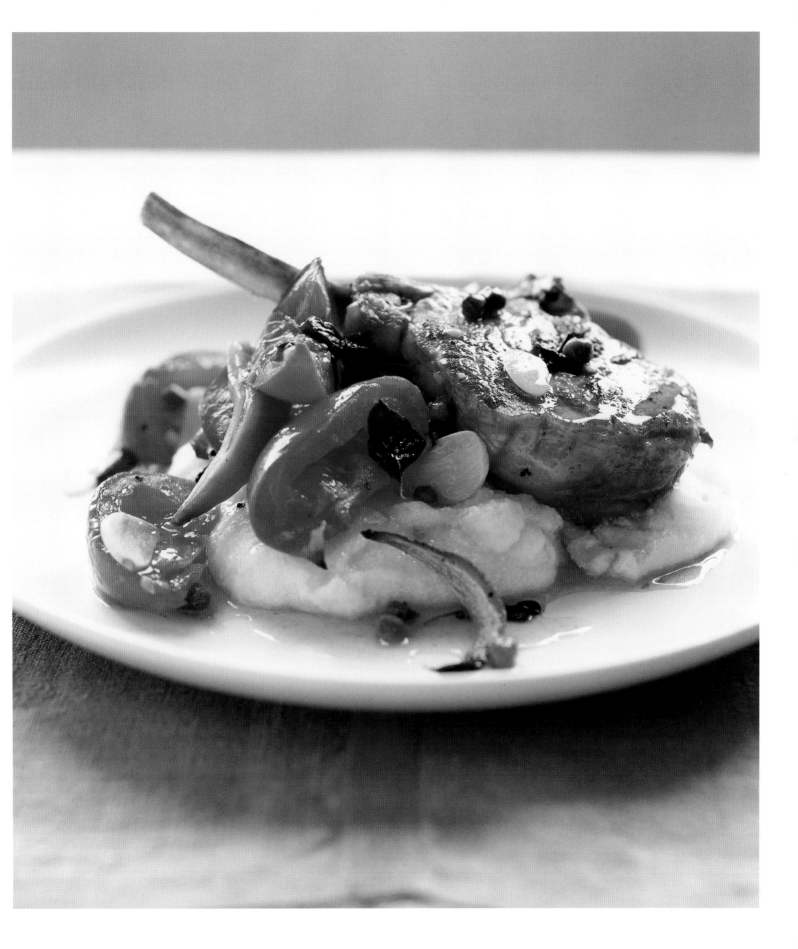

barbecued fish with preserved lemon dressing and parsley salad

4 x 1 lb 2 oz baby snappers, scaled and
cleaned
2½ tablespoons olive oil
sea salt
freshly ground black pepper

to serve
preserved lemon dressing (see below)
parsley salad (see below)

Make three diagonal slashes on both sides of each fish. Brush
the fish with olive oil and season with salt and pepper. Heat the
barbecue or broiler until very hot and cook for 4 minutes each side,
or until the fish is opaque and just cooked. Remove the fish to a
serving dish and drizzle over the preserved lemon dressing. Serve
with the parsley salad.

PRESERVED LEMON DRESSING

¼ cup extra virgin olive oil
freshly ground black pepper
4 teaspoons fresh oregano
¼ cup preserved lemon rind only, rinsed
and thinly sliced

Place the olive oil, 2½ tablespoons water and pepper in a bowl and
whisk to combine. Add the oregano and preserved lemon and stir
to combine.

PARSLEY SALAD

1 cup fine grain bulgur
½ cup finely chopped scallions
1 cup fresh Italian parsley, roughly chopped
⅓ cup olive oil
¼ cup lemon juice
1½ teaspoons ground cumin
1 fresh green chili, seeded and finely
chopped
2 Lebanese cucumbers, quartered
lengthways and thinly sliced
sea salt
freshly ground black pepper

Place the bulgur in a fine sieve over the sink. Soak the bulgur
with lots of water, and let stand for 30 minutes. Squeeze out
any remaining water before placing in a bowl with the remaining
ingredients. Season to taste with salt and pepper then stir
to combine.

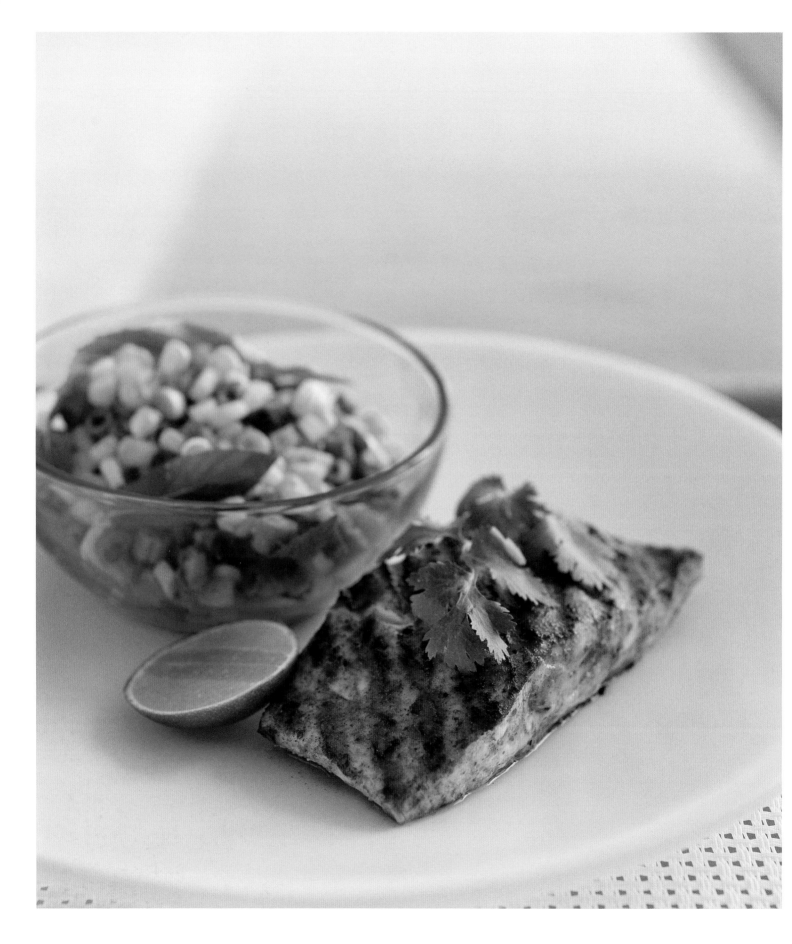

grilled white fish with corn salsa

¼ cup olive oil

1 teaspoon paprika

1 teaspoon ground cumin

4 x 7 oz firm white fish fillets, such as
blue-eye trevalla or snapper,
skin removed

sea salt

freshly ground black pepper

to serve

fresh cilantro sprigs, to garnish

corn salsa (see below)

lime cheeks

Place the olive oil, paprika and cumin in a bowl and whisk to combine. Place the fish on a plate and pour over the marinade, turning the fish so it is evenly coated. Season with salt and pepper.

Heat a barbecue or broiler and cook the fish for 2–3 minutes. Turn and cook on the other side for 2–3 minutes, or until the fish is opaque and just cooked.

Garnish with coriander sprigs and serve on individual serving plates with the corn salsa and lime cheeks.

¼ cup olive oil

2 cups fresh corn kernels

7 oz green beans, thinly sliced

sea salt

freshly ground black pepper

4 scallions, finely chopped

½ cup fresh mint leaves, whole

1 fresh green chili, chopped

2½ tablespoons lime juice

CORN SALSA

Place a frying pan over a medium to high heat and add the oil. Once the oil is hot, add the corn and beans. Season with salt and pepper and cook for 3 minutes. Place the spring onions, mint, chili and lime juice in a bowl and add the corn mixture. Stir to combine.

marinated cilantro chicken

SERVES 4 TO 6

2 small free-range chickens, approximately
2 lb 11 oz each, cut in half
2 cups fresh cilantro stems and leaves,
roughly chopped
2 teaspoons black peppercorns
2 teaspoons sea salt
3 garlic cloves
2½ tablespoons lime juice
¼ cup vegetable oil

to serve
fresh cilantro sprigs
cucumber relish (see below)
lime cheeks

Soak eight wooden skewers in cold water for 30 minutes to stop them from burning during cooking. Wash the chicken and dry it with paper towels. Slash each chicken half a few times to allow the marinade flavours to penetrate. Run a wooden skewer through the flesh of each chicken piece to secure to the joints, and place in a large baking dish.

Place the coriander, peppercorns, salt, garlic, lime juice and oil in a blender or food processor and process until smooth. Pour the marinade over the chicken pieces, rubbing well into the flesh, and cover with plastic wrap. Place in the refrigerator to marinate for 2 hours, bringing to room temperature in the last 30 minutes.

Preheat the barbecue grill to high. Place the chicken halves on the barbecue and cook, cut side down, for 6–8 minutes. Turn and cook flesh side down for a further 5–6 minutes, or until the chicken is cooked through. Alternatively, preheat the oven to 425°F. Place the chicken on a baking sheet, skin side up, and bake for 30–35 minutes. Garnish with cilantro sprigs and serve with the cucumber relish and lime cheeks.

CUCUMBER RELISH

½ cup rice vinegar or white vinegar
½ cup superfine sugar
1 Lebanese cucumber, quartered
lengthways and thinly sliced
2 red Asian shallots or ½ red onion,
thinly sliced
1 large fresh red chili, seeded and
thinly sliced

Place the vinegar and sugar in a small saucepan over a medium heat, and stir until the sugar has dissolved. Remove from the heat and cool. Pour into a bowl, add the cucumber, shallots and chili and stir to combine.

marinated lamb cutlets with pilaf

1 teaspoon crushed coriander seeds
1 teaspoon crushed fennel seeds
½ teaspoon ground cumin
¼ teaspoon dried chili flakes
3 garlic cloves, sliced
¼ cup extra virgin olive oil
sea salt
freshly ground black pepper
12 French-trimmed lamb cutlets

to serve
warm lentil and rice pilaf (see below)
ginger tomato sauce (see below)
lemon wedges

Place all the ingredients except the lamb cutlets in a bowl and stir to combine. Add the lamb to the marinade and toss to coat. Cover with plastic wrap and place in the refrigerator to marinate for 2 hours, bringing to room temperature in the last 30 minutes.

Heat a frying pan over a high heat for 1 minute. Add the cutlets and cook for 1–2 minutes, turn and cook for another minute for medium-rare. Serve with the ginger tomato sauce, warm lentil and rice pilaf and lemon wedges.

1 cup small green lentils
1 cup long-grain rice
½ lemon
2½ tablespoons extra virgin olive oil
1 large onion, finely sliced
sea salt
freshly ground black pepper
½ cup fresh Italian parsley, roughly chopped

WARM LENTIL AND RICE PILAF

Bring a large pot of water to a boil, add the lentils and cook for 10 minutes. Add the rice and lemon and cook for another 12–15 minutes, or until the lentils and rice are tender. Drain, discarding the lemon, and place in a serving bowl.

Meanwhile, heat a frying pan over a medium to high heat. When hot, add the oil and onion, and cook for 10–12 minutes, or until the onion is a rich golden brown (don't worry if it catches a bit), stirring frequently. Remove from the heat. Sprinkle the pilaf with salt, pepper, parsley and half of the cooked onion. Stir to combine. Top with the remaining onion and serve.

GINGER TOMATO SAUCE

Make this simple ginger tomato sauce by frying a little chili, ginger and garlic in olive oil until fragrant. Add 1 lb 5 oz chopped tomatoes and cook for 25 minutes.

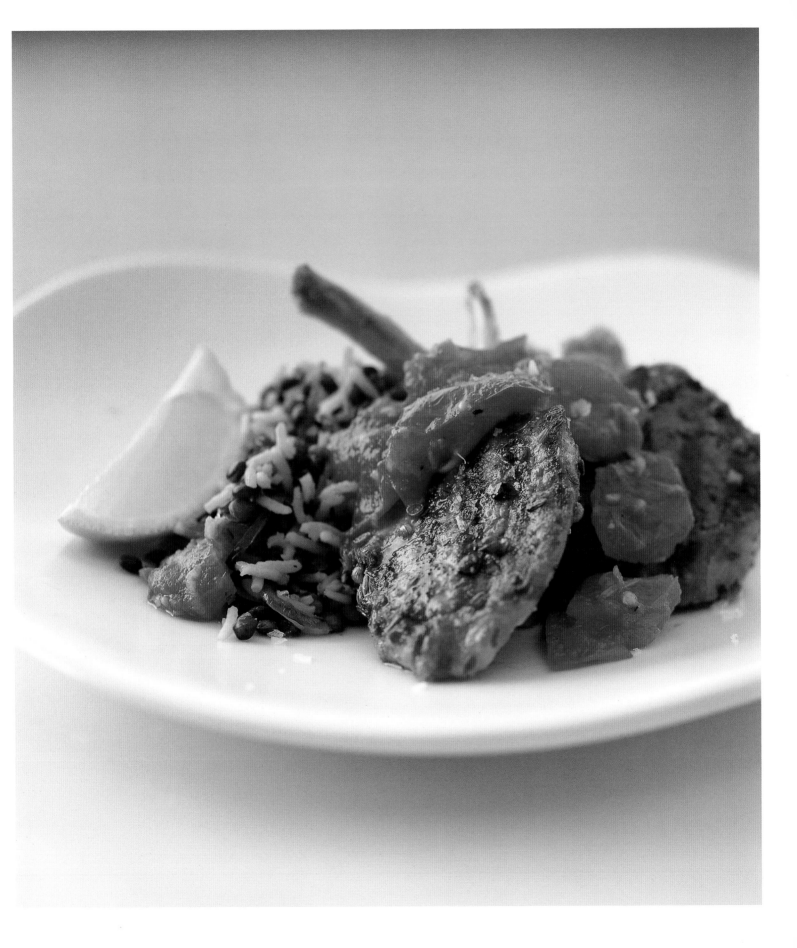

beef and mushroom pot pies with relish

SERVES 6

2½ tablespoons all-purpose flour

2 teaspoons paprika

1 teaspoon sea salt

freshly ground black pepper

3 lb 5 oz chuck or blade steak, cut into ¾ inch chunks

14 oz can chopped tomatoes

5 garlic cloves, sliced

2 red onions, halved and thinly sliced

1 celery stalk, finely chopped

1 cup red wine

1 teaspoon fresh thyme, chopped

10½ oz button mushrooms

½ cup Italian parsley, roughly chopped

13 oz block puff pastry

1 egg yolk, lightly beaten

to serve

spicy tomato relish (store-bought, or see page 47)

Preheat the oven to 350°F. Place the flour and paprika in a bowl and stir to combine. Season with the salt and pepper. Add the beef and toss until covered in flour. Place in an ovenproof casserole dish. Add the tomatoes, garlic, onion, celery, red wine and thyme and stir. Cover and cook for 1½ hours, stirring occasionally. Add the mushrooms, cover and return to the oven. Cook, stirring occasionally, for 1 hour, or until the sauce is thickened slightly and the beef and mushrooms are tender. Remove from the oven and stir through the parsley. The filling can be made up to a day in advance to this stage. Increase the oven temperature to 400°F.

On a lightly floured surface, roll out the pastry until ⅛ inch thick. Using the top of a 1½ cup ovenproof ramekin as a template, cut out six circles of pastry, leaving ½ inch extra around the circumference.

Divide the pie filling into six 1½ cup ovenproof ramekins and cover with pastry, pushing down the edges around the rim. Make a cut in the pastry top with a sharp knife to allow any steam to escape and brush with the egg yolk. Bake for 20–25 minutes or until the pastry is lightly golden and the filling is hot. Serve with spicy tomato relish.

rice noodles with shrimp and lime

SERVES 2

4½ oz dried rice noodles

10 raw shrimp, peeled, deveined and halved lengthways

2½ tablespoons korma curry paste

2½ tablespoons light-flavored oil (I like canola)

2 eggs, lightly beaten

4 scallions, cut into 2 inch lengths

½ cup chicken stock

2½ tablespoons soy sauce

to serve

fresh cilantro sprigs

lime wedges

Put the noodles in a bowl and soak in hot water for about 5 minutes or until soft. Drain well and set aside. Put the shrimp in a bowl with the curry paste and stir until the shrimp are well coated.

Heat a large frying pan or wok over a high heat. Add 4 teaspoons of the oil and pour in the eggs. Leave to set for 10 seconds, then push the eggs to the center of the pan, almost scrambling them. When the eggs are about three-quarters cooked, remove them from the pan.

Wipe out the pan or wok with paper towels and return to the heat. Add the remaining oil and the shrimp and stir gently for 1–2 minutes, then add the scallions and stir-fry for 1 minute. Add the stock, soy sauce and noodles and stir-fry for 1–2 minutes until heated through. Add the egg, toss to combine and remove from the heat. Divide between two bowls and serve with cilantro sprigs and lime wedges.

This is a dish that's very adaptable to whatever happens to be in your fridge. Chicken instead of shrimp is an easy variation.

219

baked meatballs with tomatoes

1 lb 2 oz ground beef or pork and veal
1 small onion, grated
⅔ cup fresh white breadcrumbs
¼ cup fresh Italian parsley, chopped
¼ cup cilantro leaves, chopped
1 egg, lightly beaten
1 teaspoon ground cumin
1 teaspoon sweet paprika
2 large fresh red chilies, finely chopped
sea salt
freshly ground black pepper
¼ cup olive oil
2 x 14 oz cans chopped tomatoes
½ teaspoon sugar

to serve
roast chili potatoes (see below)

Preheat the oven to 425°F. Combine the ground beef, onion, breadcrumbs, parsley, cilantro, egg, cumin, paprika, half of the chili and plenty of salt and pepper in a large bowl. Mix gently with your hands, then shape into small balls (I find wetting my hands makes this easier).

Toss the meatballs gently in the oil in a roasting pan and bake for 10–15 minutes. Transfer them to a frying pan over a medium heat and add the tomatoes, sugar, remaining chili and some more salt and pepper. Stir the meatballs carefully to coat and then simmer for 20 minutes. Serve with the roast chili potatoes.

2 lb 4 oz potatoes, peeled and roughly diced
2½ tablespoons olive oil
sea salt
1 large fresh red chili, thinly sliced
3 scallions, thinly sliced
small handful of fresh cilantro leaves, chopped

ROAST CHILI POTATOES

Preheat the oven to 425°F. Toss the potatoes with the olive oil, place on a large baking sheet and season with sea salt. Roast for 40 minutes, turning once, until golden and crispy. Scatter with the chili, scallions and cilantro leaves and return to the oven for another 2 minutes before serving.

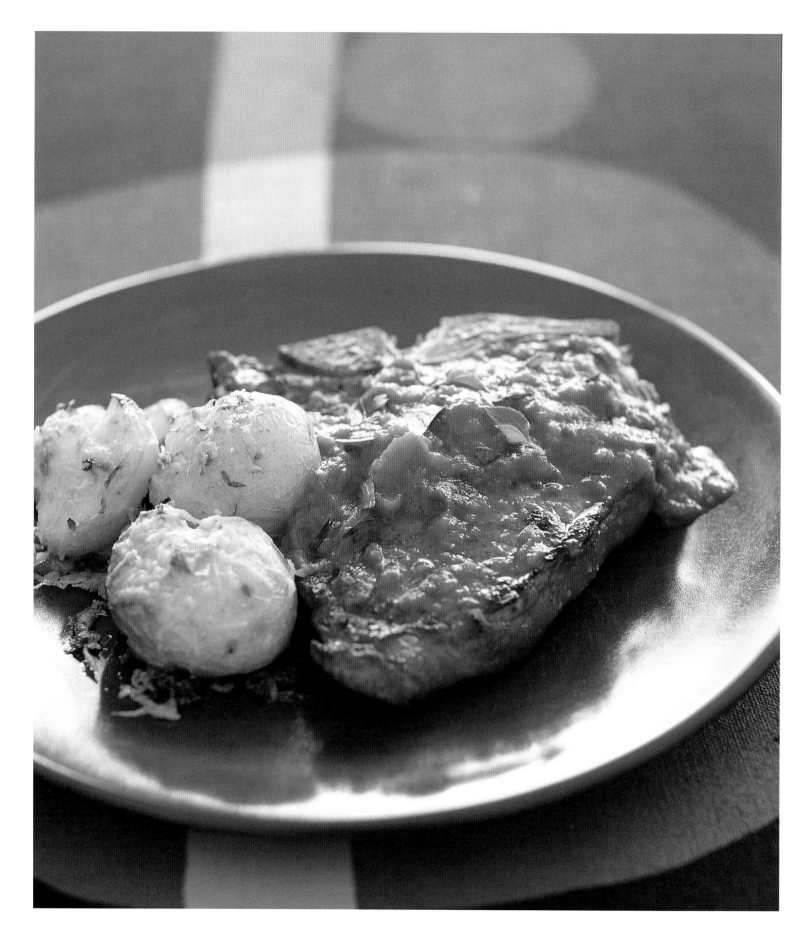

bistecca alla pizzaiola

2 T-bone steaks, ¾ inch thick
extra virgin olive oil, for brushing
sea salt
freshly ground black pepper
½ cup white wine
1 cup good-quality tomato pasta sauce
¼ teaspoon dried chili flakes
4 teaspoons fresh oregano

to serve
4 teaspoons fresh Italian parsley, chopped
crispy potatoes (see below)

Heat a large frying pan over high heat. Brush both sides of the steaks with olive oil and season well with salt and pepper. Cook the steaks for 1 minute on each side until brown, then remove from the pan and set aside. Add the wine to the hot pan and stir for 1 minute to reduce slightly. Stir in the pasta sauce, chili and oregano.

Put the steaks back in the pan, reduce the heat to medium and cook for 5 minutes, turning once. Sprinkle with parsley and serve with crispy potatoes.

CRISPY POTATOES

6 small new potatoes
sea salt
¼ cup grated parmesan cheese
2½ tablespoons olive oil
freshly ground black pepper
1 teaspoon lemon zest
1 garlic clove, crushed

Preheat the oven to 425°F. Boil the potatoes in salted water for about 15 minutes until tender. Drain and leave to cool slightly.

Put the potatoes on a baking sheet and flatten slightly with the palm of your hand (or a fork or potato masher). Mix together the parmesan, olive oil, salt, pepper, lemon zest and garlic and sprinkle over the potatoes. Bake for 25 minutes until crispy.

giovanni's sausages with potatoes and rosemary

6 Italian-style sausages
1 lb 12 oz potatoes, scrubbed and sliced
(I use kipfler/fingerling)
1½ teaspoons paprika
2 rosemary stalks
sea salt
freshly ground black pepper
½ loaf ciabatta, crust removed
1¾ fl oz extra virgin olive oil

to serve
handful fresh basil leaves
arugula leaves

Preheat the oven to 400°F. Slice the sausages thickly and place in a large roasting pan. Add the potatoes, paprika, rosemary, salt and pepper. Tear the ciabatta into bite-sized pieces and add to the pan. Drizzle with the oil and toss gently.

Roast, stirring occasionally, for 30–40 minutes or until the potatoes are tender and the sausages and bread are golden brown. Sprinkle with the basil and serve with a salad of arugula leaves.

stir-fried noodles with beef and sugar snaps

¼ cup oyster sauce

2½ tablespoons soy sauce

2 tablespoons dry sherry

¼ cup chicken stock

2 teaspoons sugar

4 teaspoons light-flavored oil
(I like canola)

14 oz beef fillet or rump, sliced

1½ inch piece of fresh ginger, julienned
or grated

7 oz sugar snap peas

to serve

9 oz fresh egg noodles

Bring a large pot of salted water to a rapid boil. Cook the noodles for 1–2 minutes or until tender, drain.

Stir together the oyster sauce, soy sauce, sherry, stock and sugar in a small bowl.

Heat a wok or large frying pan over high heat. Add the oil and, when it is smoking, stir-fry the beef in two batches, cooking for 1 minute until it is sealed and browned. Remove from the wok and set aside. Stir-fry the ginger and peas for 2 minutes, adding a little more oil if needed. Add the beef and sauce and cook for 1 minute, until the sauce has thickened slightly.

Divide the noodles among four bowls and top with the stir-fry. (Or add the noodles to the wok and mix it all together.)

crispy-skinned salmon with anchovy vinaigrette, fennel and green beans

SERVES 4

4 x 6¼ oz salmon fillets, skin on
2½ tablespoons olive oil
sea salt
freshly ground black pepper
2 baby fennel bulbs, finely sliced
9 oz baby green beans, trimmed
and blanched
small handful of fresh Italian parsley

to serve
anchovy vinaigrette (see below)

Heat a frying pan over a medium–high heat for 2 minutes. Brush the salmon with oil and season well with salt and pepper. Cook the salmon, skin side down, for 3 minutes, then turn over and cook for another minute. Remove from the pan and leave to rest for 2 minutes. The salmon should be quite rare and the skin crispy.

Arrange the fennel, beans and parsley on plates. Place the salmon on top and drizzle with anchovy vinaigrette to serve.

ANCHOVY VINAIGRETTE

I small garlic clove
4 anchovies
3½ fl oz extra virgin olive oil
1¾ fl oz red wine vinegar
freshly ground black pepper

In a mortar and pestle, pound the garlic and anchovies to a rough paste. Add the olive oil and red wine vinegar and stir together. Season with pepper (you probably won't need salt).

ocean trout with red chili and tomatoes

SERVES 4

4 teaspoons olive oil, plus a little extra

4 x 7 oz ocean trout fillets, skin on

2 large fresh red chilies, sliced

2 inch piece of fresh ginger, grated

3 garlic cloves, sliced

14 oz tomatoes, chopped

2½ tablespoons soy sauce

2 tablespoons sugar

to serve

steamed rice

baby English spinach leaves

Heat the oil in a large frying pan over a medium–high heat. Add the trout and cook for 2 minutes on each side or until cooked to your taste. Remove from the pan.

Reduce the heat to medium and add a little extra oil. Add the chili, ginger and garlic and cook for 2 minutes until golden. Add the tomatoes, soy sauce and sugar and cook for 5 minutes, stirring occasionally until thickened.

Serve the trout with steamed rice, baby English spinach leaves and the sauce spooned over the top.

230

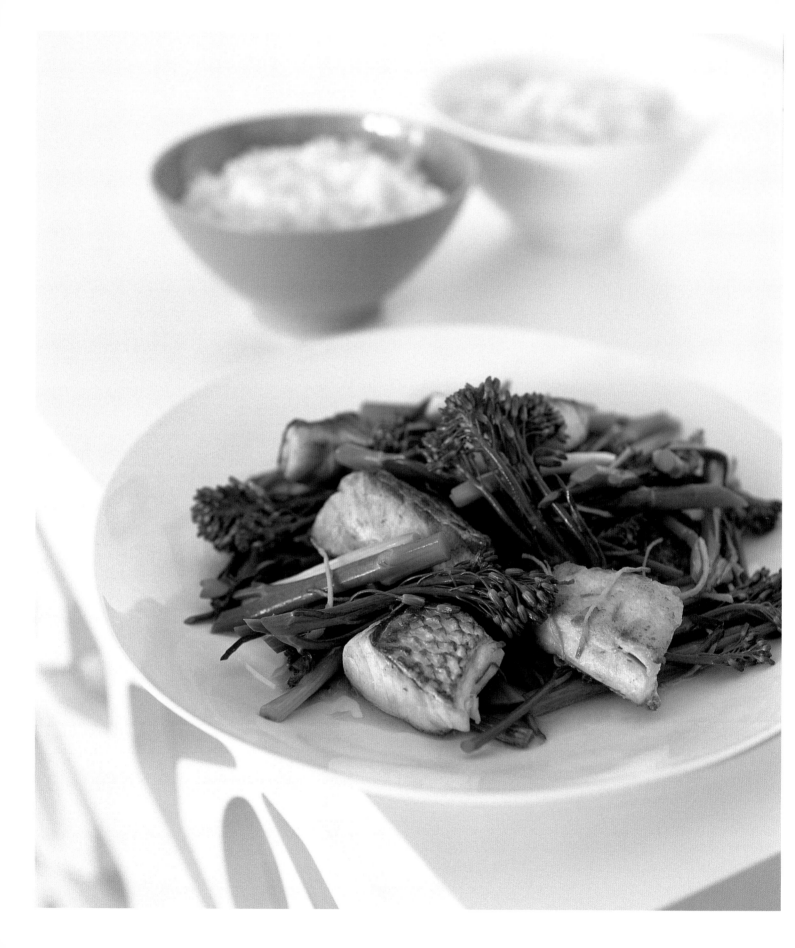

stir-fried ginger fish with broccolini

4 teaspoons light-flavored oil
(I like canola)

⅓ cup fresh ginger, julienned

12 oz firm white fish fillets, skin on (I like
blue-eye trevalla or snapper),
cut into bite-sized pieces

8 scallions, cut into long lengths

7 oz broccolini, sliced on the diagonal
and blanched

2½ tablespoons fish sauce

2 teaspoons sugar

I teaspoon sea salt

2½ tablespoons lime juice

to serve
steamed jasmine rice

Heat a wok over a medium–high heat. Add the oil and, when hot, stir-fry the ginger for 1 minute. Add the fish and stir-fry for 3 minutes. Add the spring onions, broccolini, fish sauce, sugar and salt and gently stir-fry for another minute. Remove from the heat, add the lime juice and serve with steamed jasmine rice.

To julienne ginger, choose a large piece of fresh ginger and trim to make a rectangle. Slice thinly and then cut the slices into matchsticks.

233

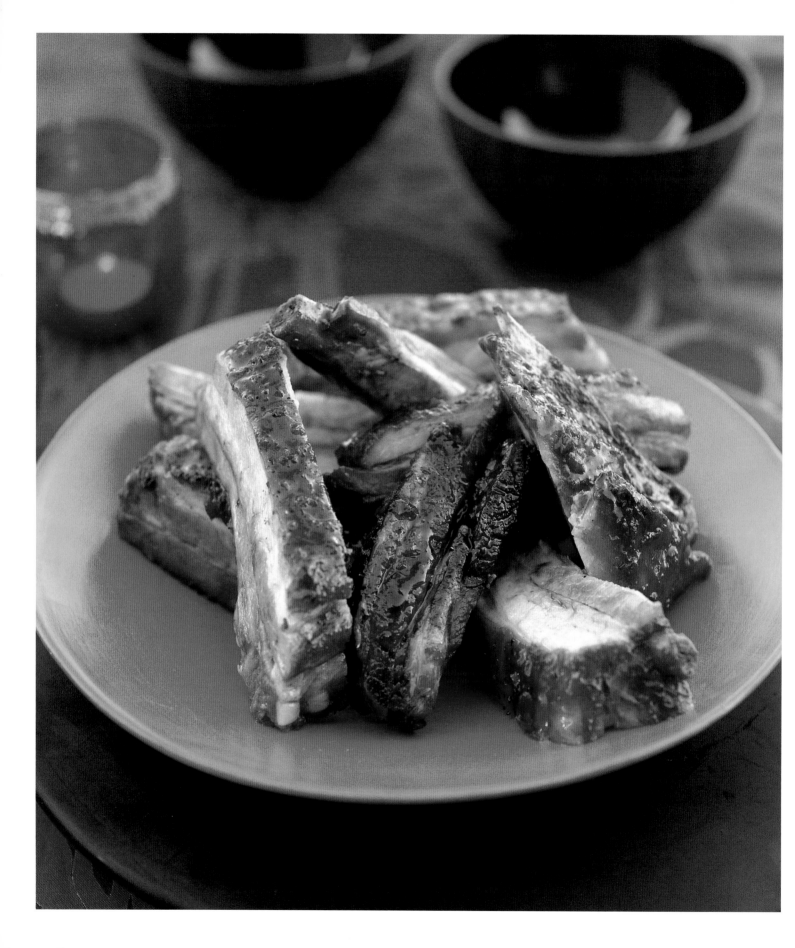

sticky spare ribs

2 pork spare rib racks (around 3 lb each)

sea salt

freshly ground black pepper

4 garlic cloves, crushed

2½ tablespoons finely grated fresh ginger

1 cup soy sauce

½ cup honey

¼ cup shaoxing rice wine, or dry sherry

1 teaspoon five-spice

½ cup hoisin sauce

to serve

snow peas, steamed

steamed rice

Preheat the oven to 315°F. Put the ribs on a baking pan and season generously with salt and pepper. Roast for 1 hour.

Meanwhile, put the garlic, ginger, soy sauce, honey, shaoxing rice wine, five-spice and hoisin sauce in a small saucepan over a medium heat and cook for 15 minutes, stirring occasionally, until thick.

Baste the ribs with the sauce and cook for another 20 minutes. Put the ribs on a chopping board, brush again with the sauce and cut into individual ribs to serve.

butterflied lamb with romesco sauce

SERVES 6

4 lb butterflied lamb leg, cut into
two pieces
¼ cup olive oil
sea salt
freshly ground black pepper

to serve
romesco sauce (see below)
virgin paella (see below)
lemon wedges
small handful of fresh Italian parsley

Preheat the oven to 350°F. Heat an ovenproof frying pan over high heat. Rub the lamb with the oil and season well with salt and pepper. Put the lamb skin side down in the pan and sear for 5 minutes, then turn over and cook for 2 minutes. Put the pan in the oven and roast for 15 minutes. Cover loosely with foil and rest for 10 minutes. Slice thickly and serve with romesco sauce, lemon wedges and parsley.

ROMESCO SAUCE

4 red peppers, roasted,
peeled and seeded
⅓ cup blanched almonds, toasted
4 teaspoons red wine vinegar
2½ tablespoons extra virgin olive oil
sea salt
freshly ground black pepper

Put all the ingredients in a blender and pulse until the sauce is combined but still has some texture.

VIRGIN PAELLA

4 teaspoons olive oil
1 white onion, chopped
2 cups paella rice
½ cup white wine
5 cups chicken stock
6 saffron threads
sea salt

Heat the oil in a large, heavy-based deep frying pan or paella pan over a low–medium heat and cook the onion for 5 minutes until soft and golden. Add the rice and cook for 1 minute, stirring to coat. Add the wine and cook for 1 minute. Add the stock and saffron and cook, stirring occasionally, for 15 minutes or until the rice is just cooked. Season with salt and serve.

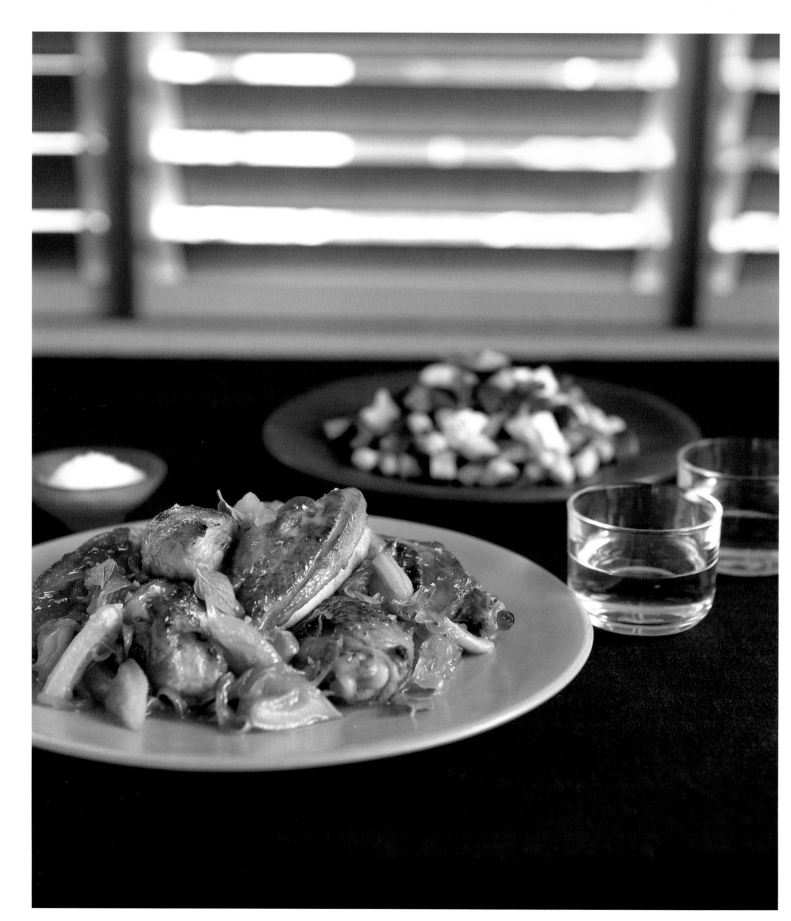

braised chicken with lemon and honey

4 teaspoons olive oil

3 lb 8 oz chicken, cut into 8 pieces

I red onion, sliced

12 garlic cloves, peeled but left whole

I lemon, cut into chunks

¾ cup chicken stock

½ cup honey

small handful of fresh oregano

to serve

shepherd's salad with feta (see below)

Heat a large frying pan over a high heat, add the oil and chicken and cook for 5 minutes until golden. Remove and set aside. Reduce the heat to medium–high, add the onion and cook for I minute. Add the garlic and cook for I minute.

Return the chicken to the pan with the lemon, chicken stock and honey, reduce the heat, cover the pan and simmer for 20 minutes or until the chicken is cooked through. Lift out the chicken and put on a baking pan. Increase the heat under the sauce, and simmer, uncovered, for another 15 minutes to thicken. Place the chicken under a hot broiler until crisp. Arrange the chicken on a platter, drizzle with the sauce and sprinkle with oregano. Serve with shepherd's salad with feta.

SHEPHERD'S SALAD WITH FETA

14 oz can chickpeas, rinsed

5½ oz feta cheese, crumbled

small handful of fresh Italian parsley

2 Lebanese cucumbers, chopped

I green pepper, chopped

⅓ cup black olives, pitted and halved

dressing

¼ cup olive oil

4 teaspoons lemon juice

sea salt

freshly ground black pepper

Gently mix together the chickpeas, feta, parsley, cucumber, pepper and olives in a large bowl. To make the dressing, whisk the olive oil and lemon juice and season with salt and pepper. Toss the dressing with the salad.

herbed chicken schnitzel

4 chicken breasts, skin removed
½ cup all-purpose flour
freshly ground black pepper
1 teaspoon sea salt
1 egg
2½ tablespoons milk
2 cups fresh breadcrumbs
¼ cup fresh Italian parsley, chopped
¼ cup fresh chervil, chopped
¼ cup fresh oregano, chopped
4 teaspoons butter
½ cup olive oil

to serve
mashed potatoes

Put each chicken breast between two sheets of plastic wrap and flatten slightly with a meat mallet or rolling pin. Cut each flattened breast in half. Put the flour in a shallow bowl and season with pepper and the salt. In a second bowl, lightly beat the egg and milk together. Mix the breadcrumbs and fresh herbs in a third bowl and season with salt and pepper. Dip each chicken fillet in flour to coat, then in the egg mixture and lastly in the breadcrumbs.

Heat the butter and olive oil in a large non-stick frying pan over a medium heat and cook the schnitzels for 3 minutes on each side until golden brown and cooked through (don't overcrowd the pan: cook them in batches if necessary). Drain on paper towels and keep warm until all the chicken is cooked.

FENNEL 'SLAW

3 fennel bulbs, thinly sliced
2½ tablespoons small salted capers, rinsed
1 small red onion, thinly sliced
2 tablespoons Italian parsley, chopped
¼ cup whole-egg mayonnaise
2 tablespoons lemon juice
sea salt
freshly ground black pepper

Put the fennel, capers, onion and parsley in a bowl. Mix together the mayonnaise and lemon juice and stir through the 'slaw. Season with sea salt and black pepper to serve.

broccolini and tofu sambal

2½ tablespoons peanut oil
13 oz firm tofu, cut into strips
1 onion, cut into thin wedges
½ teaspoon sea salt
2 garlic cloves, finely chopped
2 bunches broccolini, cut into long florets
2 teaspoons sambal oelek (optional)
2½ tablespoons light soy sauce
4 teaspoons lemon juice

to serve
steamed rice

Heat half the oil in a wok or frying pan over a high heat. Cook the tofu in batches for 2 minutes on each side until it is golden brown. Lift out of the wok and set aside.

Return the wok to high heat and add the remaining oil, onion and salt. Stir-fry for 1 minute, then add the garlic and broccolini and cook for another 2 minutes. Add the sambal oelek, if using, and soy sauce and toss through. Add the tofu and stir in the lemon juice. Serve immediately with steamed rice.

moroccan fish stew

4 teaspoons olive oil

1 large onion, thinly sliced

1 garlic clove, crushed

2 teaspoons grated fresh ginger

1 teaspoon ground cumin

1 teaspoon turmeric

1 cinnamon stick

pinch of cayenne pepper

14 oz can chopped tomatoes

sea salt

1 lb 2 oz firm white fish fillets, such as blue-eye trevalla, snapper or ling, cut into chunks

14 oz can chickpeas, rinsed

2 teaspoons honey

freshly ground black pepper

to serve
fresh cilantro leaves
flaked almonds, lightly toasted

Heat the olive oil in a large heavy-based frying pan over a medium–low heat. Add the onion and cook, stirring occasionally, for 5 minutes, or until the onion is translucent. Add the garlic, ginger, cumin, turmeric and cinnamon and cook, stirring, for 2 minutes, or until fragrant.

Add the cayenne, tomatoes, a pinch of sea salt and 1 cup of water and cook, stirring frequently, for 10 minutes. Add the fish and simmer for 5 minutes, or until the fish is just tender. Add the chickpeas and honey and cook for a further 2–3 minutes. Season to taste with salt and pepper. Serve garnished with cilantro and flaked almonds.

lime, paprika and honey glazed chicken

2½ tablespoons all-purpose flour
2 teaspoons paprika
sea salt
freshly ground black pepper
8 chicken legs
2 red onions, cut into wedges
2½ tablespoons olive oil
2½ tablespoons grated fresh ginger
I garlic clove, crushed
2½ tablespoons honey
½ cup chicken stock
I lime, cut into thin wedges

to serve
steamed rice
Asian greens
fresh cilantro leaves

Preheat the oven to 425°F. Mix the flour and paprika and season with salt and pepper. Dust the chicken legs in the flour and then put in a large roasting pan with the onions. Drizzle with the olive oil and roast for 20 minutes, turning the chicken once during this time.

Mix together the ginger, garlic, honey and chicken stock. Pour over the chicken and add the lime wedges to the pan. Roast for another 10 minutes, or until the chicken is golden and glazed.

Serve with steamed rice, Asian greens and lots of cilantro leaves.

spaghetti with garlic and spinach

SERVES 4

14 oz spaghetti

⅓ cup extra virgin olive oil

6 garlic cloves, thinly sliced

sliced fresh red chili, to taste (I like to use 2 small ones)

⅓ cup white wine

2 cups baby English spinach

to serve

sea salt

freshly ground black pepper

freshly grated parmesan cheese

Cook the spaghetti in a large pot of rapidly boiling salted water until *al dente* and drain. Meanwhile, put the olive oil, garlic and chili in a frying pan over a medium heat and cook, stirring often, for about 5 minutes until the garlic is golden. Add the wine and cook, stirring, for 20 seconds. Add the drained pasta and spinach and toss to coat it well. Season with salt and pepper, then serve with lots of grated parmesan cheese.

sausages with caramelized onions and parmesan mash

SERVES 4

4 red onions, quartered (or cut into eighths, if large)
2½ tablespoons soft brown sugar
½ teaspoon chili flakes
sea salt
freshly ground black pepper
2½ tablespoons extra virgin olive oil
2½ tablespoons red wine vinegar or balsamic vinegar
8 good-quality sausages

to serve
parmesan mash (see below)

1 lb 12 oz waxy potatoes, peeled and cut into chunks
½ cup milk
1 oz butter
⅓ cup finely grated parmesan cheese
sea salt
freshly ground black pepper

Preheat the oven to 400°F. Put the onions in a baking dish and sprinkle with the sugar, chili flakes, salt and pepper. Drizzle with olive oil and vinegar and bake for 35 minutes.

Cook the sausages in a frying pan over a medium–high heat for about 15 minutes until well browned. Serve with the caramelized onions and parmesan mash.

PARMESAN MASH

Cook the potatoes in boiling salted water until tender, then drain and mash. Heat the milk and butter in a saucepan until the butter has melted and then beat into the mash until smooth. Add the parmesan and beat well. Season with salt and pepper.

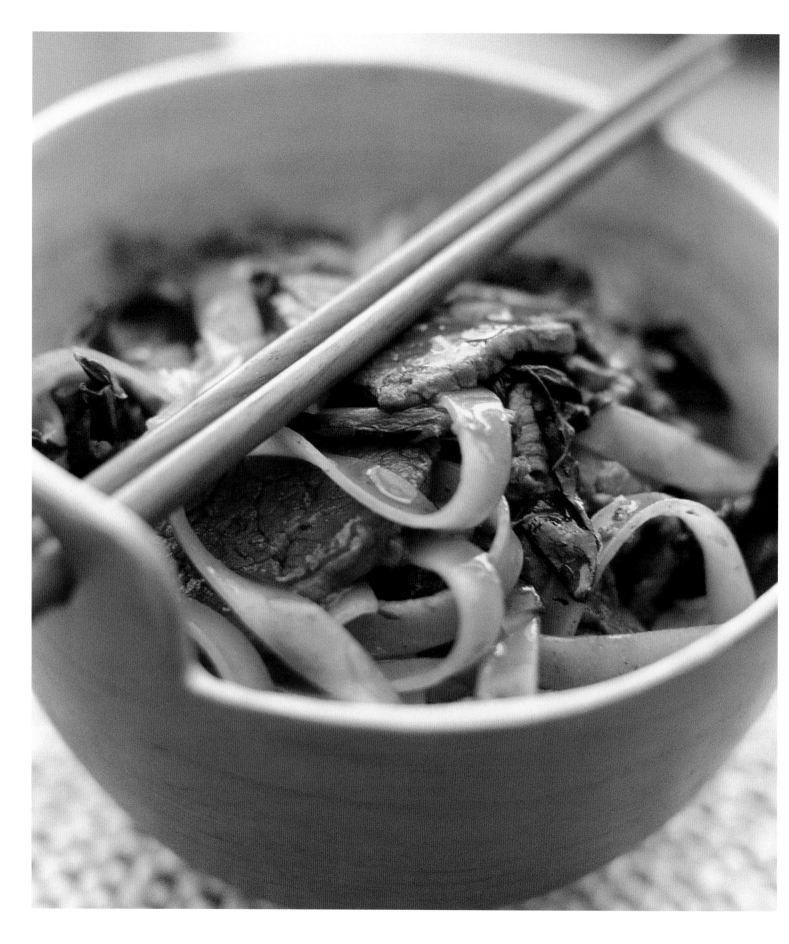

beef and noodle stir-fry with asian greens

SERVES 4

13 oz fresh rice noodles

2 teaspoons sesame oil

¼ cup oyster sauce

2½ tablespoons dark soy sauce

2 tablespoons dry sherry or shaoxing rice wine

¼ cup chicken stock

2 teaspoons sugar

4 teaspoons peanut oil

1 lb 5 oz beef fillet or rump, thinly sliced

1½ inch piece of fresh ginger, julienned or grated

1 bunch Chinese broccoli (gai larn), stalks removed and halved, leaves halved

Cover the noodles in boiling salted water according to the packet instructions. Drain and toss with the sesame oil. Meanwhile, stir together the oyster sauce, soy sauce, sherry, stock and sugar.

Heat a wok or large frying pan over a high heat. Add the peanut oil and, when smoking, add the beef in two batches, cooking for 1 minute to seal and brown. Remove and set aside. Add the ginger and Chinese broccoli, adding a little extra oil if needed, and stir-fry for 2 minutes. Add the beef and sauce and cook for another minute to slightly reduce the sauce.

Either toss the noodles through the sauce in the wok, or spoon them into bowls and top with the beef stir-fry.

253

spicy chicken meatballs

¼ cup olive oil

1 small onion, finely diced

2 garlic cloves, crushed

½ teaspoon ground coriander

1 large fresh red chili, thinly sliced

1 lb 2 oz ground chicken

¼ cup fresh breadcrumbs

1¾ oz pancetta, chopped

2½ tablespoons Italian parsley, chopped

sea salt

1 lb 2 oz cherry tomatoes, halved

freshly ground black pepper

½ cup chicken stock

to serve

1 lb 2 oz whole-wheat fusilli, cooked

parmesan cheese shavings

Preheat the oven to 400°F. Heat 4 teaspsoons of the olive oil in a saucepan over a medium-high heat. Add the onion and garlic and cook, stirring, for 5 minutes, or until the onion is soft. Add the coriander and chili and cook for 1 minute. Set aside to cool completely.

Put the chicken in a bowl with the breadcrumbs, pancetta, parsley and salt. Add the spiced onion and mix well with your hands. Refrigerate for 30 minutes to firm the mixture. Wet your hands with cold water to stop the mixture sticking and roll it into small meatballs.

Put the cherry tomatoes on a baking sheet lined with baking paper, drizzle with 4 teaspoons of the olive oil and season with salt and pepper. Put the meatballs on a second lined sheet and drizzle with the remaining oil. Roast the tomatoes and meatballs in the oven for 15–20 minutes, or until the meatballs are golden and the tomatoes are starting to pucker.

Put the stock and tomatoes in a saucepan and add the meatballs. Simmer for 5 minutes and season to taste before spooning over pasta and serving with parmesan shavings.

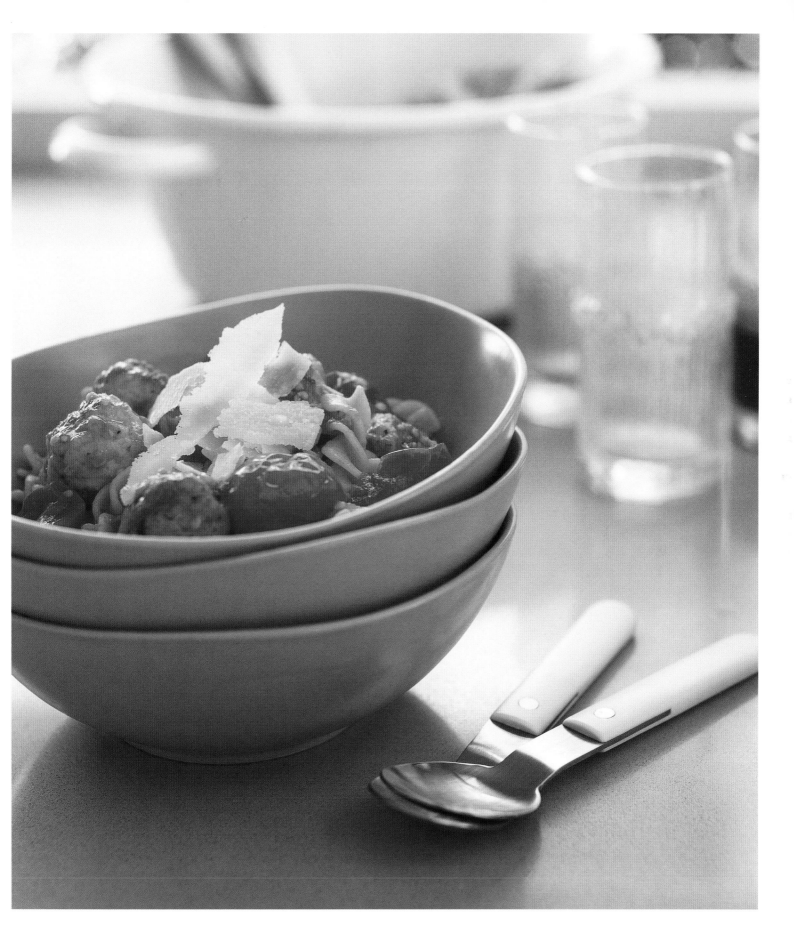

oven-baked chicken and asparagus risotto

SERVES 4

2½ tablespoons olive oil

1 lb 2 oz boneless chicken breasts, cut into thin strips

1 onion, finely chopped

1 garlic clove, crushed

1 teaspoon finely grated lemon zest

9 oz arborio rice

3 cups chicken stock

1 bunch asparagus, sliced on the diagonal

⅓ cup grated parmesan cheese, plus extra to serve

sea salt

freshly ground black pepper

Preheat the oven to 350°F. Heat half of the olive oil in a large flameproof casserole dish over a high heat. Add the chicken and cook, stirring frequently, for 3–4 minutes, or until golden brown. Remove and set aside.

Add the remaining olive oil and the onion to the casserole and cook, stirring occasionally, for 5 minutes, or until the onion is soft. Add the garlic and lemon zest and cook, stirring, for 30 seconds. Add the rice and stir to coat in the oil. Add the stock and bring to a boil, stirring occasionally.

Cover the casserole and put in the oven for 15 minutes. Add the asparagus, return the chicken to the casserole and bake for a further 3–4 minutes, or until the asparagus is bright green and just tender. Stir in the parmesan and season with salt and pepper, before serving with extra parmesan.

lamb biryani

2 lb 4 oz boneless lamb leg,
trimmed and diced
4 teaspoons garam masala
2 teaspoons ground cumin
½ teaspoon turmeric
2½ tablespoons olive oil
1 onion, thinly sliced
2 garlic cloves, crushed
2 teaspoons finely grated fresh ginger
1½ cups basmati rice
3 cups chicken stock
small handful of fresh cilantro leaves

to serve
cumin, mint and cilantro yogurt
(see below)

Preheat the oven to 400°F. Put the lamb in a large bowl with the garam masala, cumin and turmeric and toss to coat the lamb in the spices. Heat half of the oil in a flameproof casserole over a medium heat, add the lamb in batches and cook, stirring occasionally, for 3–4 minutes until browned all over, adding a little more oil if necessary. Remove and set aside.

Add the remaining oil, onion, garlic and ginger to the casserole dish and cook over a medium heat until the onion is soft and pale golden. Add the rice, stir together and cook for 2 minutes. Return the lamb to the casserole in a single layer and carefully pour in the stock. Put the lid on the casserole and put in the oven. Cook for 35–45 minutes, or until the rice is tender and has absorbed all the liquid. Top with cilantro leaves and serve with cumin, mint and cilantro yogurt

CUMIN, MINT AND CILANTRO YOGURT

10 oz natural yogurt
1 teaspoon ground cumin
2½ tablespoons finely fresh mint, chopped
2½ tablespoons fresh cilantro leaves,
finely chopped
¾ inch piece of fresh ginger, grated
large fresh green chili, seeded and finely
chopped
sea salt
freshly ground black pepper
lightly toasted cumin seeds

Stir together the yogurt, cumin, mint, cilantro, ginger and chili. Season well with salt and pepper and sprinkle with cumin seeds. Serve as an accompaniment to curries.

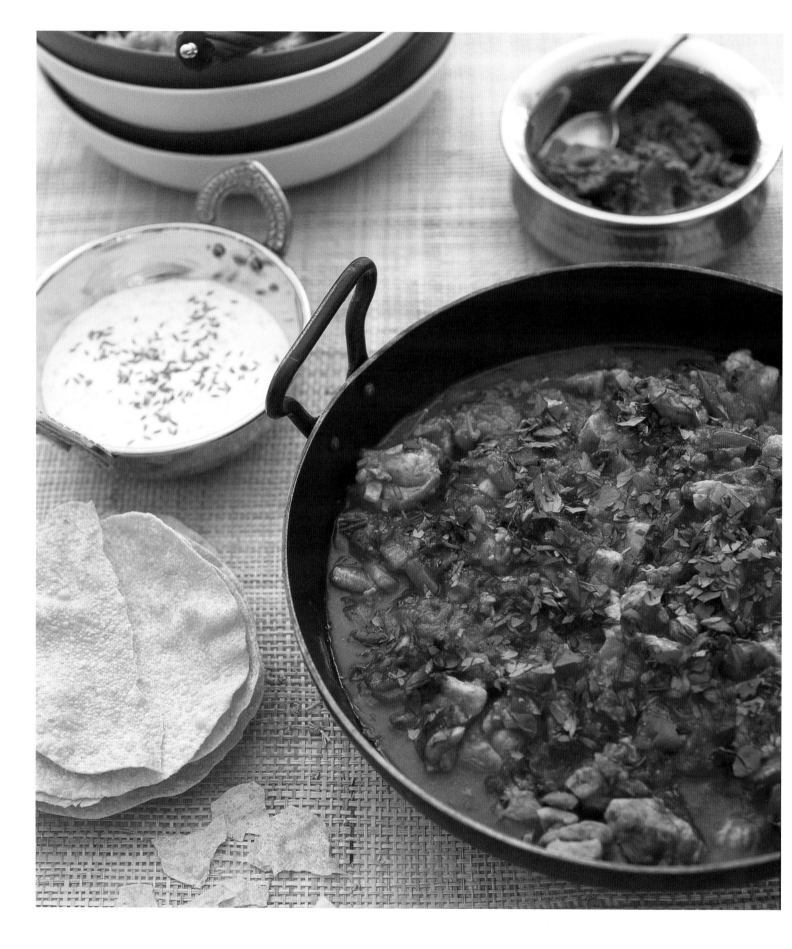

fragrant chicken and spinach curry

2½ tablespoons vegetable oil

1 large onion, chopped

2 teaspoons ground coriander

½ teaspoon turmeric

pinch of cayenne pepper

2 garlic cloves, crushed

4 teaspoons grated fresh ginger

1 lb 10 oz boneless chicken thighs, cubed

14 oz can chopped tomatoes

½ teaspoon sea salt

2 teaspoons soft brown sugar

4 teaspoons lime juice

2 cups baby English spinach, finely chopped

large handful of fresh cilantro leaves, chopped

to serve

steamed rice

Heat the oil in a large heavy-based frying pan over a medium heat. Add the onion and cook, stirring, for 5–6 minutes until the onion is soft. Add the spices, garlic and ginger and cook, stirring, for 2 more minutes. Add the chicken and increase the heat to medium-high. Cook, stirring often, for 5 minutes, or until the chicken is browned.

Stir in the tomatoes and salt and bring to simmering point. Reduce the heat to low, cover the pan and simmer gently for 15 minutes. Add the sugar, lime juice and spinach and stir until the spinach has just wilted. Remove from the heat, sprinkle with cilantro and serve with steamed rice.

ricotta- and herb-stuffed roast chicken

SERVES 4

3 lb 8 oz free-range chicken
1½ cups fresh ricotta cheese
2½ tablespoons fresh chives, snipped
2½ tablespoons fresh chervil, chopped
2 teaspoons finely grated lemon zest
sea salt
freshly ground black pepper
olive oil

Preheat the oven to 400°F. To spatchcock the chicken, place the bird, breast side down, on a chopping board. Using poultry shears or a sharp knife, cut along both sides of the backbone, cutting through the skin and bone. Remove the backbone. Turn the bird over and press firmly on the breast bone to break the bone and flatten the breast. Tuck the wing tips under the breast.

Mix together the ricotta, herbs, lemon zest, salt and pepper. With your fingers, carefully loosen the skin over the breast of the chicken and down to the thigh area. Spread the ricotta mixture evenly under the skin to cover the breast and thigh.

Put the chicken in a roasting pan, drizzle with olive oil and season with salt and pepper. Roast for 50 minutes, or until the juices run clear when you insert a skewer into the thickest part of the thigh. Leave to rest for 5 minutes before carving.

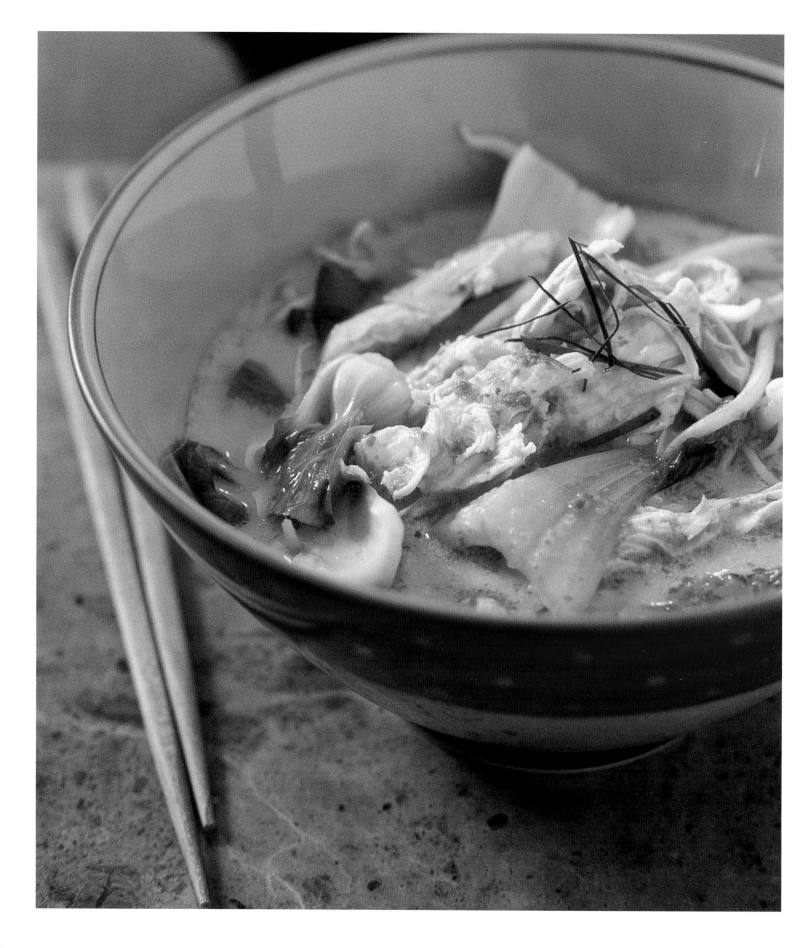

SERVES 4 # light laksa

1 teaspoon peanut oil
4 teaspoons red curry paste
4 cups chicken stock
5 fl oz coconut milk
2 kaffir lime leaves, plus extra leaves, thinly sliced, to garnish
1¼ inch piece of fresh ginger, sliced
1 lb 2 oz boneless chicken breasts
5½ oz rice vermicelli
soft brown sugar and lime juice, to taste
1 bunch baby bok choy, leaves separated
1 cup trimmed bean sprouts

Heat the oil in a large saucepan over a medium heat. Add the curry paste and cook, stirring, for 1–2 minutes, or until fragrant. Add the stock, coconut milk, lime leaves and ginger.

Increase the heat to high and bring to a boil. Then reduce the heat to very low, add the chicken, cover the pan and poach the chicken gently for 7 minutes, or until just cooked through. Remove the chicken and set aside to cool slightly, then shred.

Put the rice vermicelli in a bowl and pour in enough boiling water to cover. Soak for 6–7 minutes, then drain.

Season the soup with the brown sugar and lime juice, to taste. Divide the rice vermicelli, shredded chicken, bok choy and bean sprouts among four large bowls. Pour in the hot soup and garnish with thinly sliced lime leaves.

white bean and chorizo soup

1 teaspoon olive oil
1 chorizo sausage (about 5½ oz), diced
1 large onion, thinly sliced
2 celery stalks, diced
2 garlic cloves, crushed
2 teaspoons fresh thyme, chopped
1 teaspoon paprika
2 tomatoes, diced
4 cups chicken stock
2 x 14 oz cans cannellini beans, rinsed
sea salt
freshly ground black pepper

Heat the olive oil in a large saucepan over a high heat and cook the chorizo for 3–4 minutes until crisp. Drain on paper towels.

Reduce the heat to medium-low, add the onion and celery to the pan and cook, stirring occasionally, for 6–7 minutes until softened. Add the garlic, thyme and paprika and cook, stirring, for 1–2 minutes until fragrant. Add the tomatoes and cook for another minute.

Return the chorizo to the pan with the stock and bring to the boil, then reduce the heat and simmer, stirring occasionally, for 10 minutes. Add the beans and cook for another 5 minutes. Season with salt and pepper before serving.

dessert

Desserts are one of the real pleasures that have been sacrificed in an effort to cram more into a day. To me, dessert is something to linger over. It provides the ideal moment for savoring the day and incites some of the best compliments!

Sweet things have a bad reputation but I'm a great fan of moderation and there's nothing wrong with the occasional bit of butter and sugar. As a cook, nothing gives me more satisfaction than making sweet things for people to enjoy.

I adore pleasing people and dessert is a sure-fire way to anyone's heart.

honey cheesecake

SERVES 8

½ cup golden raisins

¼ cup Marsala, or cold weak tea

¼ cup superfine sugar

6 eggs

finely grated zest of 1 orange

¼ cup honey

2 lb 4 oz good-quality ricotta cheese, lightly mashed to break up any lumps

confectioners sugar, for dusting

to serve

1 cup raspberries

Preheat the oven to 315°F. Place the raisins and Marsala in a small bowl and leave to soak for 30 minutes.

Place the sugar and eggs in a large bowl and beat for 5 minutes, or until light and foamy. Drain the raisins then fold through the egg mixture with the zest, honey and ricotta until combined.

Pour the batter into a 9 inch greased or non-stick springform cake pan. Bake for 1 hour, or until golden. The cake will wobble slightly in the center.

Remove from the oven and leave to cool in the pan. Transfer the cake onto a serving platter, dust with confectioners sugar and serve with the raspberries.

Because this cake is so simple, I love to use fresh ricotta cheese cut from a wheel rather than from a tub. If you do find that your ricotta is watery, leave it to drain in a strainer for 30 minutes before using.

yogurt pannacotta with rose-scented plums

1½ cups cream
½ cup superfine sugar
1 vanilla bean, split lengthways
¼ oz sachet of powdered gelatin
2 cups skim milk yogurt

to serve
rose-scented plums (see below)

Place the cream and sugar in a saucepan over a medium heat. Using the point of a knife, scrape the vanilla bean seeds into the saucepan before adding the entire bean. Stir until the sugar is dissolved, then just bring to the boil before removing from the heat. Discard the vanilla bean. Pour ½ cup of the cream mixture into a small bowl, sprinkle the gelatin powder over the top and whisk with a fork until smooth. Pour back into the saucepan and stir until the gelatin has completely dissolved. (If you wish to use gelatin leaves instead, follow the manufacturer's instructions.) Add the yogurt and whisk until smooth. Strain the mixture through a fine strainer and divide between eight ½ cup molds, cover with plastic wrap and chill for 3 hours, or until just set.

To serve, dip each mold into hot water for a few seconds, making sure the water only comes halfway up the sides. Place a plate on top and invert the pannacotta. Serve immediately with the rose-scented plums and a spoonful of plum syrup.

ROSE-SCENTED PLUMS

1½ cup superfine sugar
4 teaspoons rosewater
8 ripe plums, sliced

Place the sugar and rosewater into a large deep frying pan with 2 cups water.

Stir gently over a low heat until the sugar dissolves. Increase the heat to high and bring the syrup to the boil. Boil rapidly for 1 minute then add the plums. Allow the syrup to come back to the boil then reduce to a simmer. Cook, stirring occasionally, for 8–10 minutes, or until the fruit is tender. Remove the plums, increase the heat and boil the syrup for a few minutes or until reduced. Pour over the plums and allow to cool before serving.

chocolate self-saucing pudding

SERVES 4

1 cup all-purpose flour
a pinch of salt
½ cup superfine sugar
1 tablespoon baking powder
⅓ cup cocoa powder
1 cup milk
3 oz unsalted butter, melted
2 eggs, lightly beaten
1 teaspoon natural vanilla extract

topping
1 cup soft brown sugar
2½ tablespoons cocoa powder
1 cup boiling water

to serve
thick cream

Preheat the oven to 350°F. Sift the flour, salt, sugar, baking powder and cocoa powder into a bowl. Add the milk, butter, egg and vanilla and mix with beaters until combined. Pour into four 1-cup greased pudding molds.

To make the topping, stir the brown sugar and cocoa powder in a bowl to combine, then sprinkle it over the pudding batter.

Pour ¼ cup boiling water carefully and evenly over each pudding, then bake for 20–25 minutes. Serve with thick cream.

mandarin and almond cake

3 mandarins, unpeeled and scrubbed
1 cup superfine sugar
6 eggs
2 cups ground almonds

caramelized citrus zest
1/4 cup superfine sugar
zest of 2 oranges
lightly whipped cream

Put the mandarins in a medium-sized saucepan and cover with water. Bring to a boil and simmer for 2 hours, adding water when necessary to keep the mandarins covered at all times.

Preheat the oven to 315°F. Drain the mandarins and cool to room temperature. Once cooled, split them open with your hands and remove any seeds.

Purée the mandarins, including the skins, in a food processor.

Whisk the sugar and eggs together in a large bowl until combined. Add the ground almonds and mandarin purée and stir thoroughly.

Pour the mixture into a well-greased 9 inch spring-form cake pan and bake for 1 hour 10 minutes, or until the cake looks set in the middle, springs back when touched and comes away from the edges. Remove from the oven and allow to cool in the pan.

To make the caramelized citrus zest, put the sugar in a saucepan with 1/4 cup of water over a low heat and stir until the sugar dissolves. Add the orange zest and boil the mixture until it just starts to caramelize. Lift the zest out with a fork and cool it on a plate. Serve the cake with lightly whipped cream and the caramelized citrus zest.

chocolate brownies with ice cream and warm chocolate sauce

SERVES 8

1½ cups superfine sugar
⅔ cup cocoa powder
½ cup all-purpose flour
1 teaspoon baking powder
4 eggs, beaten
7 oz unsalted butter, melted
2 teaspoons natural vanilla extract
1 cup dark chocolate buttons

to serve
good-quality vanilla ice cream
cocoa powder, for dusting (optional)
warm chocolate sauce (see below)

Preheat the oven to 315°F. Stir the sugar, cocoa powder, flour and baking powder together in a bowl. Add the eggs, melted butter and vanilla and mix until combined. Mix in the chocolate buttons. Pour into a lined 9 inch square pan and bake for 40–45 minutes.

Allow the brownie block to slightly cool then cut into eight pieces. Place on serving plates with a scoop of vanilla ice cream. Dust with cocoa powder if you like, then serve with the chocolate sauce.

WARM CHOCOLATE SAUCE

4½ oz good-quality dark chocolate, chopped
¾ cup cream

Put the chopped chocolate and the cream in a heatproof bowl and place the bowl over a saucepan of just simmering water. Whisk occasionally until a thick sauce forms. Cool slightly before serving.

apple and almond puddings

SERVES 6

5½ oz unsalted butter

5½ oz superfine sugar

3 granny smith apples, peeled, cored and sliced

I teaspoon natural vanilla extract

batter

6 oz unsalted butter, cubed

6 oz superfine sugar

3 eggs

I cup ground almonds

3½ oz all-purpose flour

2 teaspoons baking powder

I teaspoon cinnamon

to serve

cream

Preheat the oven to 350°F. Place a saucepan over a medium to high heat and add the butter and sugar. Stir until the butter is melted and the sugar dissolved. Add the apple and vanilla and cook for 10 minutes, or until soft and caramelized.

To make the batter, cream the butter and sugar until pale and creamy. Add the eggs, one at a time, stirring until well combined. Fold in the ground almonds, flour, baking powder and cinnamon and mix until combined.

Lightly grease and line six 1-cup ovenproof ramekins. Arrange the caramelized apples on the bottom. Divide the batter evenly between the ramekins and smooth over with the back of a spoon. Cook for about 25 minutes, or until lightly golden.

Run a knife around the edge of each ramekin then invert onto a serving dish. Serve with cream.

chilled zabaglione

6 egg yolks
⅓ cup superfine sugar
¾ cup Marsala
finely grated zest of 1 lemon
½ teaspoon natural vanilla extract
¾ cup cream, lightly whipped

to serve
lady fingers cookies (optional)

Whisk the egg yolks, sugar, Marsala, lemon zest and vanilla in a heatproof bowl over a saucepan of simmering water for about 5–6 minutes, or until the mixture is light and frothy. Remove from the heat and allow to cool. Fold in the lightly whipped cream, then pour into four glasses or a serving dish. Chill for at least 2 hours.

Serve with lady finger cookies, if you wish.

It is really important to not leave the stove for this recipe — you don't want scrambled eggs!

blueberry trifle

¼ cup superfine sugar

4 teaspoons lemon juice

9 oz blueberries

5 eggs, separated

½ cup superfine sugar, extra

I vanilla bean, split lengthways, or

I teaspoon natural vanilla extract

9 oz mascarpone

½ pandoro, or I sponge cake, cut into

1½ inch slices

¾ cup Marsala

½ cup flaked almonds, toasted

Place the sugar, lemon juice and ¼ cup water in a small saucepan over a medium heat. Stir until the sugar is dissolved then bring to the boil. Add the blueberries, reduce the heat to low and simmer for 5 minutes. Leave to cool.

While the syrup is cooling, place the egg yolks and extra sugar in a bowl and beat until the mixture is pale and creamy. Using the point of a knife, scrape the vanilla bean seeds and add to the bowl. Add the mascarpone and beat until smooth.

Place the egg whites in a clean, dry stainless steel bowl and whisk until soft peaks form. Using a large metal spoon, fold lightly through the mascarpone mixture in two batches.

Line a 8 cup serving bowl with a layer of pandoro or sponge cake, moisten with roughly a quarter of the Marsala, top with a quarter of the blueberries and syrup, and a quarter of the mascarpone mixture. Repeat the layering, reserving 2 tablespoons of the blueberries and syrup for garnishing, until you finish with a layer of the mascarpone mixture. Cover and refrigerate for 6 hours, or overnight, to allow the flavor to develop.

Remove the trifle from the refrigerator, drizzle over the reserved blueberries and syrup, and sprinkle with toasted flaked almonds.

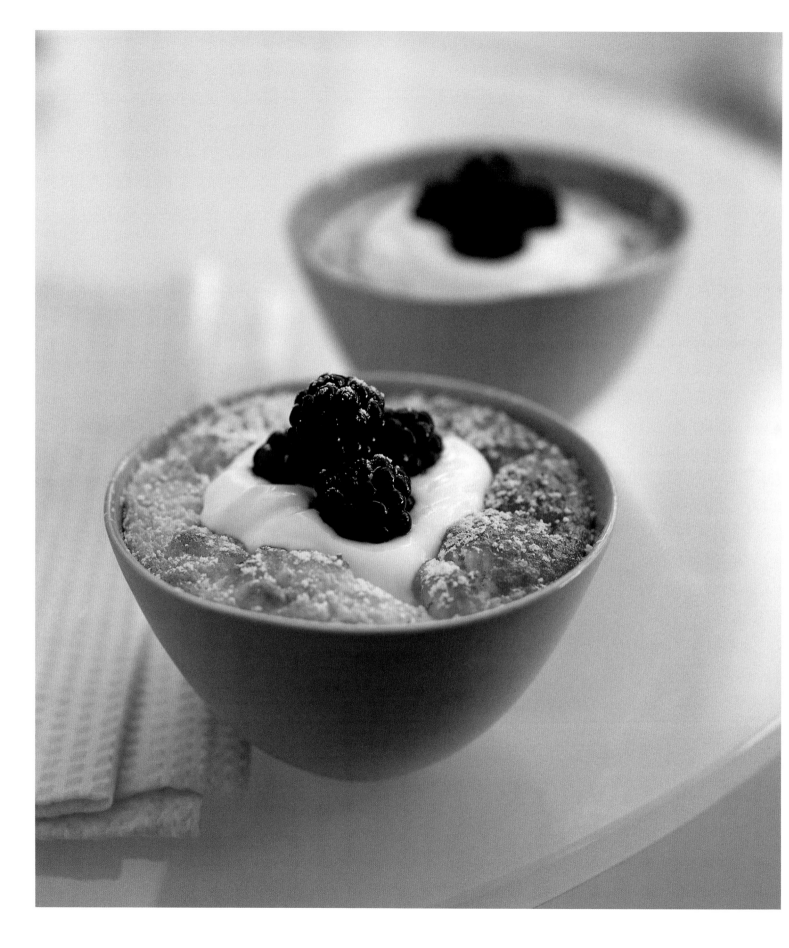

little lemon puddings with yogurt and blackberries

1¾ oz unsalted butter
finely grated zest of 1 lemon
½ cup superfine sugar
2 eggs, separated
⅓ cup all-purpose flour, sifted
1¼ cups milk
2½ tablespoons lemon juice

to serve
plain yogurt
9 oz blackberries
confectioners sugar, for dusting

Preheat the oven to 350°F. Place the butter, zest and sugar in a bowl and beat until pale and creamy. Add the egg yolks, one at a time, beating well after each addition. Fold through the flour then gradually add the milk in a steady stream, whisking lightly to combine. Add the lemon juice and mix to combine. The mixture will look slightly curdled.

Place the egg whites in a clean, dry stainless steel bowl and whisk until stiff peaks form. Using a large metal spoon, fold lightly through the pudding batter. Pour the batter into four 1-cup ovenproof ramekins and place on a baking pan. Bake for 15 minutes, or until lightly browned. Place a dollop of yogurt and the blackberries on top then dust with confectioners sugar.

apple and passionfruit crumble

6 granny smith apples, peeled and
thinly sliced
½ cup sugar
pulp from 8 passionfruit

topping
1 cup old-fashioned oats
⅔ cup soft brown sugar
⅓ cup all-purpose flour
3½ oz butter, softened

to serve
vanilla ice cream or thick cream

Preheat the oven to 350°F and grease an 8 cup (70 fl oz) baking dish. Mix together the apples, sugar and passionfruit pulp and put in the dish.

Using your fingertips, rub together the oats, brown sugar, flour and butter to make a crumbly topping. Sprinkle over the fruit and bake for 25–30 minutes until golden. Serve with ice cream or cream.

pistachio cake with orange blossom syrup

SERVES 10

1 cup pistachio nuts

6 eggs, separated

1 cup superfine sugar

¾ cup plain yogurt

½ cup light-flavored oil
(I like light olive or canola)

5½ oz all-purpose flour

1 teaspoon baking powder

a pinch of salt

to serve

orange blossom syrup (see below)

figs, halved

plain yogurt

Preheat the oven to 350°F. Butter and flour a 10 inch spring-form pan and line the base with parchment paper. Finely grind the pistachios in a food processor. Beat the egg yolks and half the sugar until pale and very thick. Fold in the yogurt and oil. Sift the flour, baking powder and salt over the mixture and fold through with the ground pistachios.

Beat the egg whites until soft peaks form. Gradually add the remaining sugar and beat until firm peaks form. Gently fold half into the cake mixture, then fold in the other half. Pour into the pan and bake for 30 minutes. Cover loosely with foil and bake for another 15 minutes, until a skewer inserted into the center comes out clean. Leave to cool completely in the pan and then spoon orange blossom syrup over the top. Serve with fresh figs and yogurt.

ORANGE BLOSSOM SYRUP

1 cup superfine sugar

½ cup freshly squeezed orange juice

½ teaspoon orange blossom water

Put the sugar, orange juice and ½ cup of water in a saucepan over a low heat and stir to dissolve. Increase the heat and boil for 10–12 minutes, or until syrupy. Remove from the heat and stir in the orange blossom water. Spoon over the cake while the syrup is still warm.

SERVES 6 crema catalana

2½ cups cream
⅔ cup milk
2 teaspoons natural vanilla extract
2 cinnamon sticks
peel from 1 orange
peel from 1 lemon
6 egg yolks
⅓ cup superfine sugar
3½ tablespoons soft brown sugar

Preheat the oven to 275°F. Put the cream, milk, vanilla, cinnamon, orange and lemon peel in a saucepan over a medium heat and bring just to boiling point, then remove from the heat.

Whisk together the egg yolks and superfine sugar in a large bowl. Strain the cream and pour slowly over the yolk and sugar mixture, whisking constantly. Skim off any foam that rises to the top.

Put six ½-cup ramekins in a large roasting pan and spoon the mixture into the ramekins. Pour hot water into the pan to come halfway up the sides of the ramekins and cover the whole pan with foil. Bake for 30–35 minutes, or until just set. Lift the ramekins out of the roasting pan and leave to cool before chilling in the fridge for 2 hours.

Preheat the broiler to its hottest temperature. Put the ramekins on a baking sheet, sprinkle brown sugar over the chilled creams and then place under the broiler for a couple of minutes until the sugar is melted and dark golden (if you have a chef's blowtorch, this is the time to use it). Leave for a few minutes for the sugar to cool and harden before serving.

295

pavlova with yogurt cream and strawberries

SERVES 8

6 egg whites
¼ teaspoon cream of tartar
1 teaspoon natural vanilla extract
1⅓ cups superfine sugar
4 teaspoons cornstarch
2½ tablespoons arrowroot
2 teaspoons white vinegar

to serve
1 cup cream, whipped
½ cup plain yogurt
1⅔ cup strawberries, hulled and halved, if large
4 teaspoons confectioners sugar

Preheat the oven to 350°F and line a baking pan with parchment paper. Draw a circle on the paper about 8 inches in diameter.

Beat the egg whites, cream of tartar and vanilla in a clean, dry bowl until stiff peaks form. Add the sugar, a tablespoon at a time, beating continuously until the meringue is glossy and thick. Stir in the cornstarch, arrowroot and vinegar.

Pile the meringue onto the circle on the baking pan and put in the oven. Immediately reduce the oven to 235°F and bake the pavlova for 1 hour 20 minutes, or until the outside is firm but not browned. Turn off the oven and leave the pavlova inside, with the door ajar, until completely cooled.

Gently fold together the cream and yogurt. Toss the strawberries with the icing sugar. Spoon the yogurt cream over the pavlova and top with strawberries to serve.

white chocolate mousse with raspberry ripple

9 oz good-quality white chocolate, chopped
⅓ cup milk
1 teaspoon natural vanilla extract
3 eggs, separated
1½ cups cream
2 cups raspberries

Place the white chocolate, milk and vanilla in a heatproof bowl over a saucepan of simmering water, making sure the bowl does not touch the water. Heat until the chocolate is just melted, stirring regularly. Allow to cool for 5 minutes. Add the egg yolks, beating well after each addition.

Whip the cream in a bowl until soft peaks form then fold through the chocolate mixture until just combined. Whisk the egg whites in a large, dry, clean stainless steel bowl until soft peaks form. Using a large metal spoon, fold through the chocolate mixture in two batches. Divide the mousse between six 1-cup serving dishes. Using a fork, crush the raspberries in a separate bowl then swirl over the top of the mousse. Cover and chill for 3 to 4 hours, or until set.

This mousse is just as delicious with fresh passionfruit or crushed blackberries swirled in.

MAKES 12 raspberry tarts

1 cup superfine sugar
10½ oz fresh raspberries
2 cups all-purpose flour
1 cup confectioners sugar
a pinch of salt
6½ oz unsalted butter, chilled
and cubed
¼ cup iced water
¾ cup mascarpone
¾ cup cream, lightly whipped
1 teaspoon vanilla bean paste

To make a raspberry syrup, put the superfine sugar in a pan with ¼ cup of water and stir over a low heat to dissolve the sugar. Increase the heat and bring to a boil. Cook until golden, then remove from the heat. Mash 3½ oz of the raspberries and stir into the syrup. Leave to cool.

Sift the flour, confectioners sugar and salt in a bowl and stir to combine. Using your fingertips, rub in the butter until the mixture resembles coarse breadcrumbs. Add the iced water and mix until the dough comes together in a ball. Wrap in plastic wrap and chill for 30 minutes. Roll out on a lightly floured surface until ⅛ inch thick, then press lightly into 12 individual tart pans and prick with a fork. Chill for a further 30 minutes.

Preheat the oven to 400°F. Line the chilled pastry with parchment paper and add the baking weights or uncooked rice. Bake for 10 minutes, then remove the paper and weights. Bake for another 10 minutes, or until the pastry is golden and crisp. Leave to cool.

Remove the pastry cases from the pans and arrange on a serving plate. Mix together the mascarpone, cream and vanilla bean paste and spoon into the tarts. Arrange the rest of the raspberries on top and drizzle with the raspberry syrup.

raspberry, pistachio and rosewater semifreddo

SERVES 6 TO 8

6 egg yolks
¼ cup honey
1 cup cream, whipped
2 teaspoons rosewater
5½ oz fresh raspberries, plus a
few extra to serve
¼ cup pistachio nuts, chopped

Beat the egg yolks and honey together with electric beaters for 10 minutes, or until thick, pale, creamy and doubled in volume. Fold in the whipped cream and rosewater until just combined.

Line the base and two sides of an 8 x 4 inch loaf pan with a piece of plastic wrap, leaving the wrap hanging over the sides of the pan. Spoon the mixture into the pan, fold the plastic over the top to cover the semifreddo and freeze for 1–2 hours, or until partially frozen. Remove from the freezer and stir through the raspberries and pistachios. Cover with plastic wrap and return to the freezer until completely frozen.

Before serving, leave to soften in the fridge for 20 minutes. Turn out of the pan, cut into slices and serve with a few extra raspberries.

sticky date cake with butterscotch sauce

SERVES 10

1⅔ cups pitted dates, chopped
1 teaspoon baking soda
2½ oz unsalted butter, diced
¾ cup superfine sugar
1 teaspoon natural vanilla extract
2 eggs, lightly beaten
1½ cups self-rising flour, sifted

to serve
butterscotch sauce (see below)
vanilla ice cream

Preheat the oven to 350°F. Grease and line the base of a 8 inch round cake pan with parchment paper.

Put the dates in a saucepan with 1 cup of water. Cook, stirring occasionally, for 5–6 minutes until the dates are soft and all the water has been absorbed. Remove from the heat and then stir in the baking soda and butter. Set aside for 10 minutes to cool slightly.

Transfer to a large mixing bowl, add the sugar, vanilla and eggs and stir well. Fold in the sifted flour until combined. Spoon into the pan and bake for 50 minutes, or until a skewer inserted into the center comes out clean. Leave in the pan for 5 minutes, then turn out and cool on a wire rack. Serve with warm butterscotch sauce and ice cream.

BUTTERSCOTCH SAUCE

1 cup soft brown sugar
7 fl oz cream
5½ oz unsalted butter

Heat the sugar, cream and butter in a saucepan over a medium heat, stirring to dissolve the sugar. Bring to a simmer and cook over a low heat for 3 minutes. Pour over the sticky date cake to serve. Makes 2 cups.

306

cherry tart

pastry

4½ oz unsalted butter, melted and cooled

3¼ oz superfine sugar

6 oz all-purpose flour

a pinch of salt

2½ tablespoons ground almonds

filling

⅔ cup cream

2 eggs, lightly beaten

2 teaspoons natural vanilla extract

¼ cup superfine sugar

2½ tablespoons all-purpose flour

1 lb 4 oz cherries, halved and pitted (fresh are best)

to serve

cream or ice cream

Preheat the oven to 350°F and grease a 9½ inch round loose-based tart pan. To make the pastry, stir together the butter and sugar in a large mixing bowl. Add the flour and salt and stir to make a soft dough. Transfer the dough to the pan and press evenly into the base and side of the pan with your fingertips. Put the pan on a baking sheet and bake for 12–15 minutes, or until the pastry is slightly puffy. Remove from the oven and sprinkle the ground almonds over the base.

Meanwhile, to make the filling, whisk together the cream, eggs, vanilla and sugar. Add the flour and whisk until well mixed. Arrange the cherries, slightly overlapping, over the pastry base and pour the cream filling evenly over the cherries.

Return the tart to the oven for a further 40–50 minutes until the filling is firm. Leave to cool and serve with cream or ice cream.

coconut rice pudding with caramelized pineapple

SERVES 4

14 fl oz coconut milk
2 cups milk
1 cup arborio rice
¼ cup superfine sugar
1 teaspoon natural vanilla extract

to serve
caramelized pineapple (see below)

Preheat the oven to 325°F and then lightly grease an 8 × 8 inch baking dish.

Put the coconut milk, milk, rice, sugar and vanilla in the dish and stir together well. Cover with foil and bake for 1¼ hours, then remove the foil and return to the oven for another 30–35 minutes, until nicely browned on top. Leave to rest for 10 minutes before serving with caramelized pineapple.

CARAMELIZED PINEAPPLE

½ teaspoon ground cinnamon
2½ tablespoons soft brown sugar
3 thin slices fresh pineapple, cut into small triangles

Mix together the cinnamon and sugar on a large plate. Toss the pineapple triangles in the cinnamon sugar, so they are coated on all sides.

Heat a large non-stick frying pan over a medium-high heat and cook the pineapple for 1 minute on each side or until caramelized. Serve with the rice pudding.

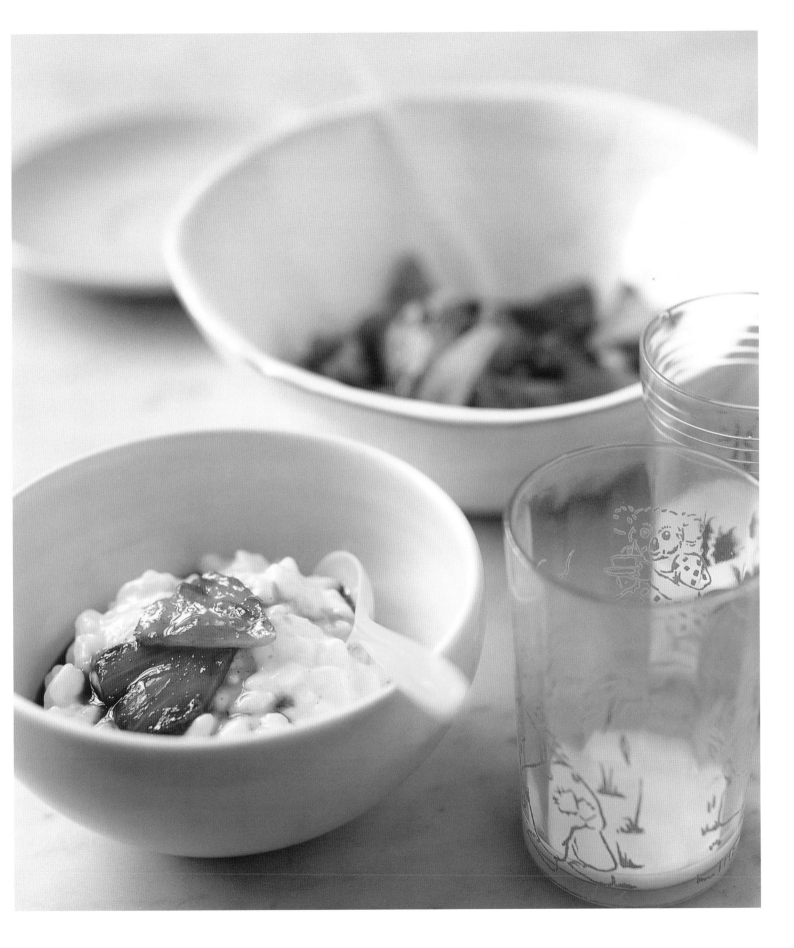

baked lemon lime tart with fresh strawberry salad

SERVES 8 TO 10

4 eggs
¾ cup superfine sugar
½ cup cream
⅓ cup lemon juice
⅓ cup lime juice
baked "9 inch" sweet shortcrust pastry shell
(see below) or ready-made shortcrust
pastry shell

to serve
1⅔ cups strawberries, hulled and
cut into quarters
4 teaspoons honey
4 teaspoons Cointreau (optional)
thick cream (optional)

Preheat the oven to 315°F. Place the eggs and sugar in a bowl and whisk to combine. Add the cream then the lemon and lime juices and whisk lightly until just combined. Pour the mixture into the cooled pastry shell and bake for 25–30 minutes, or until just set. Remove from the oven and leave to cool. Place the strawberries, honey and Cointreau, if using, into a bowl and toss gently to combine. Leave to sit for 20 minutes. Serve with the tart and thick cream, if desired.

BAKED SWEET SHORTCRUST PASTRY SHELL

2 cups all-purpose flour
1 cup confectioners sugar, sifted
a pinch of salt
6¼ oz unsalted butter, chilled
and cubed
¼ cup iced water

Place the flour, confectioners sugar and salt into a bowl and stir to combine. Using your fingertips, rub the butter through until the mixture resembles coarse breadcrumbs. Add the water and mix until the dough comes together in a ball. Shape into a round, wrap in plastic wrap and chill for 30 minutes. Roll out on a lightly floured surface until ⅛ inch thick. Press into a greased or non-stick 9 inch tart pan and prick the pastry with a fork. Chill for a further 30 minutes.

Preheat the oven to 400°F. Line the chilled pastry with parchment paper and add baking weights or rice. Bake for 15 minutes, then remove the paper and weights. Bake for another 10 minutes, or until golden and crisp. Leave to cool.

Index

Text copyright © Bill Granger 2011

Design copyright © Murdoch Books Pty Limited 2011

Photography copyright © Petrina Tinslay 2002, 2003, 2005, 2006, 2007 and © Steve Brown 2011

Lyons Press is an imprint of Globe Pequot Press

Library of Congress Cataloging-in-Publication Data is available on file

ISBN 978-0-7627-7975-8

Printed in China

10 9 8 7 6 5 4 3 2 1

IMPORTANT: Those who might be at risk from the effects of salmonella poisoning (the elderly, pregnant women, young children and those suffering from immune deficiency diseases) should consult their doctor with any concerns about eating raw eggs.

OVEN GUIDE: You may find cooking times vary depending on the oven you are using. For fan-forced (convection) ovens, as a general rule, set the oven temperature to 35°F lower than indicated in the recipe.